YOUR LOVE STARS

For Beth, my (take a deep breath)
cousin, god-daughter, friend and
fellow birthday girl, with much love

Published by OH Editions
20 Mortimer Street
London W1T 3JW

Text © Jane Struthers
Design © OH Editions

ISBN 978-1-91431-738-5

Publisher: Kate Pollard
Design: Evi O. Studio | Kait Polkinghorne
Illustrations © Evi O. Studio | Kait Polkinghorne
Production: Rachel Burgess

Repro: p2d

A CIP catalogue record for this book is available from the British Library

Printed and bound in China

10 9 8 7 6 5 4 3 2 1

JANE STRUTHERS

YOUR LOVE STARS

Unlock the secrets to compatibility,
love and better relationships

OH EDITIONS

Contents

Introduction

Think of your astrological birth chart as a snapshot of the heavens at the moment you were born, set for the place of your birth at the exact moment that you took your first breath. It's your personal blueprint, showing your whole character, including your potentials, abilities, strengths and weaknesses – and much more besides.

One of the main areas that your birth chart highlights is your capacity to give and receive love, and that's the focus of *Your Love Stars*. This book will give you greater insight into your own unique way of handling relationships and the role that love plays in your life.

What sort of love are we talking about? Everything! From sex, romance, family bonds and friendships to the connections you have with colleagues and anyone else you see on a regular basis, including your neighbours and even your pets. You'll learn whether you're best suited to close and intense relationships, easy-going and freedom-loving connections or something in between. You'll also realize that your chart shows that you have a gift for specific ways of expressing your love and affection, while others won't come naturally to you. For many of us, life is pretty much all about our relationships, so any information that can help us to improve our links with others can be very helpful. It's like being given a special key that can help us to unlock the secrets of how we get along with the people in our lives and what we expect from them.

Although *Your Love Stars* explores your love profile through the lens of astrology, you don't have to be an astrologer to use the book. It doesn't even matter if you're completely new to astrology because I'll be guiding you every step of the way. What's more, I will be zeroing in on just two of the planets that have the most effect on love and relationships, rather than your entire astrological birth chart, which helps to simplify the process of learning and understanding. Together, we'll be looking at Venus – which is the planet of love, affection, enjoyment and harmony – and Mars – which is the planet of sex, motivation, assertiveness and anger.

Introducing your birth chart

Before we go any further, let's talk briefly about your birth chart. As I've already mentioned, it is a picture of the sky at the moment you entered the world. Your chart marks the positions of the ten planets in our solar system at that exact moment in time, each of which was moving in an anticlockwise direction through one of the twelve signs of the zodiac when you were born. The ten planets are the Sun, the Moon, Mercury, Venus, Mars, Jupiter, Saturn, Uranus, Neptune and Pluto, and the twelve signs are Aries, Taurus, Gemini, Cancer, Leo, Virgo, Libra, Scorpio, Sagittarius, Capricorn, Aquarius and Pisces.

Natal chart

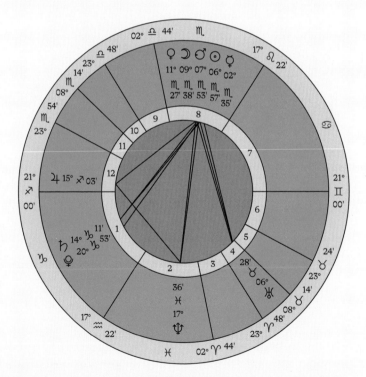

Your birth chart contains the positions of all the planets at the time of your birth

In addition, each planet occupies a segment of your chart known as a house – and this describes a particular area of life. You understand the meaning of each planet in your chart by combining its sphere of influence with the sign it occupies and, if you have an accurate birth time, the house that contains it. However, interpreting your chart doesn't stop there. Some of the planets in your chart will be separated by a specific number of degrees, meaning that they are forming what are called aspects. You can think of these aspects as being a relationship between the two planets. It might be an easy-going connection or it could be one that is hard to manage. Your birth chart is full of useful information about you, and as you begin to decode it you will be able to build your self-knowledge step by step. Just take it gently – you don't have to become a skilled astrologer overnight!

Remember, in *Your Love Stars* we are focusing on Venus and Mars, so we'll be exploring what the positions of your particular Venus and Mars signs mean for your character and your life. At the back of the book is a series of tables that will enable you to identify your own Venus and Mars signs, and then you can use that information while reading the rest of the book. For instance, you might have been born with Venus in Aquarius and Mars in Pisces, giving you a very specific astrological blueprint that will define the way you handle relationships with other people and your expectations of love and social connections. *Your Love Stars* will help you to decode and understand this information, not only about the signs that your Venus and Mars occupy in your chart but also how they work together. And, equally importantly, how they work in combination with the Venus and Mars signs of the people in your life. We will also take a look at the combination of your Sun sign with your Venus and with your Mars. Putting all this information together will help you to improve your relationships and gain a greater understanding of the way you connect with those around you.

Working with Venus and Mars

You need to harness the energies of both Venus and Mars if you want the sort of successful relationships that are described by your particular combination of those planets. While you're doing this, it's helpful to bear in mind that one person's way of relating isn't always another's. Maybe you long for a settled and emotionally secure life as one half of a couple, yet the person you're attracted to feels stifled whenever things get too cosy and predictable. Or perhaps you work with someone who's fuelled by ambition and expects you to be equally driven, whereas you prefer to keep a much more modest profile. How do you cope with that? Discovering the astrology of the situation can give you some valuable clues.

When comparing your Venus with a partner's Mars, remember that some combinations are more challenging than others but none of them is doomed to failure. You might even find that a difficult combination is a huge success because you have to work at it, whereas an apparently perfect pairing soon runs out of steam because it's too easy and eventually gets boring.

As you read this book, you can expect to have a few 'aha' moments when areas of your partnerships that have always puzzled you are finally explained. This is especially true if you've only ever explored the meaning of your Sun or Moon sign but don't know anything about the rest of your chart. You've embarked on a fascinating journey!

Part one

The Astronomy of Venus and Mars

This section of the book introduces you to the astronomy of Venus and Mars, so you can understand a little more about their orbits as well as how they relate to the other planets in the solar system.

Venus and Mars are two of the planets that can easily be seen by the naked eye, so it's fun to spot them against the stars in the evening or early morning. They are both in the list of the top five brightest objects in the sky, making them easy to find when you know where to look. The best way to locate them is with the help of an app, a website or an annual guide to the night sky. You can simply put in your location to create a map of the stars to follow. The Sun is the brightest heavenly body, followed by the Moon, Venus, Jupiter and Mars. You don't have to become an astronomer to work with the astrological energies of Venus and Mars, but seeing them laid out among the stars is a thrilling experience, transforming them from an abstract idea into something real and possibly even magical.

✳ The solar system

When you were a child, did you ever write your address as being not only your street, town and country, but also planet Earth, the solar system, the Milky Way and finally the universe? If so, you've already tapped into the knowledge that even though our world seems perfectly stable, in reality we're living on a huge rock that's continually spinning through space at breathtaking speed.

Of course, planet Earth is only one of the planets that occupy our solar system, which takes its name from the fact that it is organized around the Sun, which is classified as a yellow dwarf star. Our Sun is only one of billions of stars spread across our galaxy.

The planets in our solar system

Before the invention of the telescope in the 17th century, astronomers and astrologers were only able to study the seven heavenly bodies visible to the naked eye: the Sun, the Moon, Mercury, Venus, Mars, Jupiter and Saturn. With the exception of the Sun and Moon, which astrologers know aren't planets but which in astrology we refer to as such, the planets were all named after Roman gods and one goddess. When more planets were discovered, each of them was also given the name of a Roman god – Uranus, Neptune and Pluto (demoted to the status of a dwarf planet in 2006).

Originally, it was believed that the Sun, Moon and planets revolved around the Earth, so the Italian astronomer Galileo caused outrage in 1614 when he publicly supported the theory of Nicolas Copernicus, the Polish astronomer, that every planet revolved around the Sun. This completely contradicted the teachings of the Catholic Church, and in 1633 Galileo was found guilty of heresy. His initial sentence of life imprisonment was eventually commuted to permanent house arrest. Galileo died in 1642 but it wasn't until 1992 that the Vatican publicly acknowledged that Galileo had been right all along.

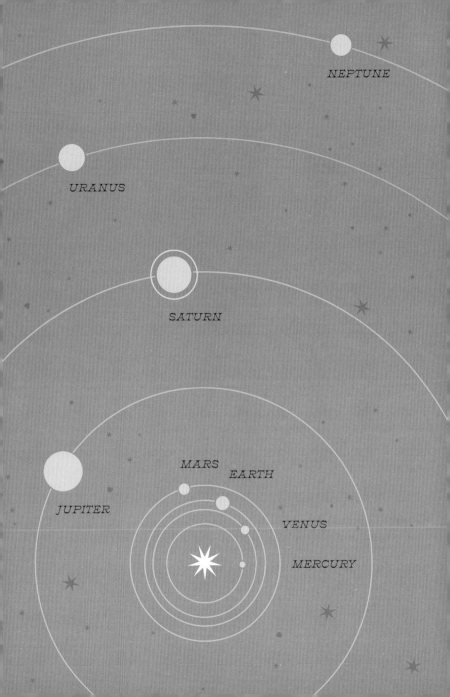

The zodiac

From our vantage point on Earth, all the planets travel through the sky along the same path as that taken by the Sun. This is called the path of the ecliptic. In order to successfully monitor the movements of the planets, early astronomers divided the ecliptic into twelve 30° sections, each of which was named after a nearby constellation. These twelve sections form the zodiac: Aries, Taurus, Gemini, Cancer, Leo, Virgo, Libra, Scorpio, Sagittarius, Capricorn, Aquarius and Pisces. As a planet travels through a particular section of the ecliptic, it is said to be in the sign named after that section. So if you were born on 29 July, when the Sun was moving through the Leo section, you were born with the Sun in Leo. Equally, if the tables at the back of this book tell you that your Venus is in Libra and Mars in Sagittarius, this means that Venus was passing through the Libra section of the sky and Mars was in the Sagittarius section when you were born.

As the planets orbit the Sun, they do not spin vertically but each is inclined on a different axis. The axis of the Earth is 23.45° from the vertical.

At some points in their passage across the heavens, some planets appear to be moving backwards in the sky. This is known as retrograde, and has an impact on your love stars. I will explain all about this later on (see page 40).

The astronomy of Venus

Astrologically speaking, Venus is the planet of beauty and love, so you might be forgiven for assuming that the planet itself must be equally lovely. Rather like the pearlescent Moon, perhaps? The truth is very different.

Astronauts have been to the Moon several times but it would take a very brave and well-equipped space traveller to set foot on Venus, even though space missions have been exploring it since the early 1960s. As you are about to discover, it's a very inhospitable place.

Type of planet
Terrestrial, which means it's similar in structure to the Earth, with a solid core surrounded by a rocky mantle

Surface temperature
Approximately 465°C (900°F), making Venus the hottest planet in the solar system

Atmosphere
Toxic, being largely composed of carbon dioxide, with droplets of sulphuric and hydrochloric acid

Atmospheric pressure
97 times higher than that on the Earth

Rotation
Venus spins backwards, so the Sun rises in the west and sets in the east

Axis
177.3°, which is quite extreme when you consider that the Earth's axis has an inclination of 23.45°

Orbit
It takes roughly one year for Venus to travel around the Sun

Retrograde period
Venus is retrograde (apparently moving backwards compared to the Earth) for no more than 43 days each year, although in some years it doesn't turn retrograde at all

Moons
None

Missions to Venus

On 4 February 1961, the USSR (as the Russian Federation was then known) launched the world's first mission to Venus. Unfortunately, the probe (*Tyazhely Sputnik*, known in the West as *Sputnik 7*) never left the Earth's orbit. The first successful attempt was when *Mariner 2*, launched by the US, managed a fly-by of Venus on 14 December 1962. The first soft landing on Venus (and indeed on any planet) was achieved by the USSR craft *Venera 7* on 15 December 1970, although the probe was damaged on landing so couldn't send back as much data as they anticipated. Many more missions have taken place since then, although no spacecraft can spend long on the surface because of the dangers of overheating and subsequent electrical failure. Japan launched its own Venus programme in 2010, and the European Space Agency (ESA) began theirs in 2018.

The morning or evening star

Venus is often referred to as the morning or evening star because it can sometimes be visible in the west at sunset and at other times is only visible in the east around dawn. This is because Venus is never more than 47° from the Sun, so they travel around the ecliptic in tandem. Sometimes Venus is ahead of the Sun, meaning that it rises or sets before the Sun, and at other times it follows the Sun. Whenever Venus and the Sun appear to be close together from our vantage point on Earth – even though in reality they are separated by an average of 108 million km (67 million miles) – the bright rays of the Sun make it impossible for us to see Venus.

Venus and mythology

The ancient Greeks created a pantheon of gods who, between them, ruled the universe, and each one had power over a particular domain, including physical substances, such as metal, as well as emotions and time. Then the Roman civilization grew to prominence and, as well as appropriating many of the Greek cultural traditions, they took over their gods, too. But although these gods retained the same qualities, they were given new names. When astronomers named the planets, they used the names of the Roman gods rather than those of the Greeks.

Here are the Roman and Greek equivalents of the gods for whom the planets were named.

Roman	Greek
Terra (Earth)	Gaia
Mercury	Hermes
Venus	Aphrodite
Mars	Ares
Jupiter	Zeus
Saturn	Cronus
Uranus	Caelus
Neptune	Poseidon
Pluto	Hades

The planet we call Venus was named for the Roman goddess of love. She was married to Vulcan, a crippled blacksmith, but was also the lover of Mars, the god of war. Ironically, Vulcan worked with iron, which is the metal ruled by Mars.

The days of the week are words we use all the time without considering their meaning, yet their origins are fascinating. In Europe, each day of the week was named after a god or goddess associated with the seven visible planets. Venus ruled over the sixth day of the week, as shown by the etymology of the relevant name in each language. It is known as Friday in the English language (from 'Frigg's day' – Frigg was the Norse goddess of love), *fredag* in Danish and *Freitag* in German (both from the same root). More obviously, the French *vendredi*, Spanish *viernes*, Italian *veneridi* and Dutch *vrijdag* all come from the Latin *Veneris dies* – 'day of the planet Venus'.

The astronomy of Mars

Mars is the fifth brightest body in the night sky and once you locate it, using your app and by its distinctive colour, you realize why it's called the red planet. Most scientists believe that the red glow is caused by the iron oxide on the surface of Mars, although the reasons for the presence of this chemical compound are still a mystery.

Here are some salient facts about the planet Mars.

Type of planet
Terrestrial, with a silicate mantle surrounding a metallic core

Surface temperature
An average of -62°C (-81°F), so it is bitterly cold

Atmosphere
Mostly carbon dioxide with a little water vapour

Atmospheric pressure
Approximately 0.6 per cent of the atmospheric pressure on Earth

Rotation
Mars spins in a forward direction

Axis
25°, which is very similar to the Earth's tilt

Orbit
Mars completes its journey around the zodiac every 17–23 months

Retrograde period
During its orbit, Mars turns retrograde only once and remains retrograde for 58–82 days

Moons
Two, called Deimos (panic) and Phobos (fear) after the two sons of Ares, the Greek equivalent of Mars

Missions to Mars

David Bowie once asked if there was life on Mars, echoing a sentiment that has occupied many scientists for centuries. They not only want to know if Mars could sustain life but if there had been life on the planet in the past. Many exploratory missions have been launched since the first (failed) one by the USSR on 10 October 1960. Several other countries have attempted to send spacecraft to Mars, including the US, UK, China, Japan and the UAE. NASA's *Mariner 4* mission performed the first successful fly-by of Mars on 15 July 1965, and NASA's *Viking 1* mission achieved the first successful landing on Mars on 20 July 1976. Many missions have taken place since then. February 2021 was particularly busy: on 9 February the UAE's *Hope* orbiter entered Mars's orbit to study its climate; on 10 February, China's *Tianwen-1* entered Mars's orbit; and on 18 February NASA's *Perseverance* rover landed on Mars to study its rocks. On 14 May 2021, China became the second nation to successfully land a spacecraft on Mars, when its *Zhurong* rover landed on the planet. One of its tasks is to search for pockets of water on Mars.

Mars, mythology and moons

In Roman mythology, Mars was immensely powerful, ranking second in importance only to Jupiter who was the ruler of the gods. The Romans celebrated festivals in Mars's honour each March and October, which demonstrates the close links between astrology and tradition: Mars is the ruler of the sign Aries, which runs from mid-March to mid-April, and is also the traditional ruler of Scorpio, the sign which runs from late October to late November.

The Greek equivalent of Mars was Ares, who lacked his Roman counterpart's popularity and was barely worshipped by the Greeks. Nevertheless, he is still remembered because the two moons of Mars were named after his two sons Phobos (fear) and Deimos (panic). These two satellites have such irregular shapes – they are distinctly lumpy – that they may not be moons at all but asteroids that have been trapped within Mars's orbit. Every day of the week corresponds with a particular planet and Mars is associated with Tuesday. In English and northern European countries, the day is named after Týr, who was a Germanic god associated with Mars. This gives us Tuesday in English and *tirsdag* in Danish. The Latin *dies Martis* ('day of Mars') is the root of the name of the third day of the week in many Romance languages, including *mardi* in French, *martes* in Spanish and *martedì* in Italian.

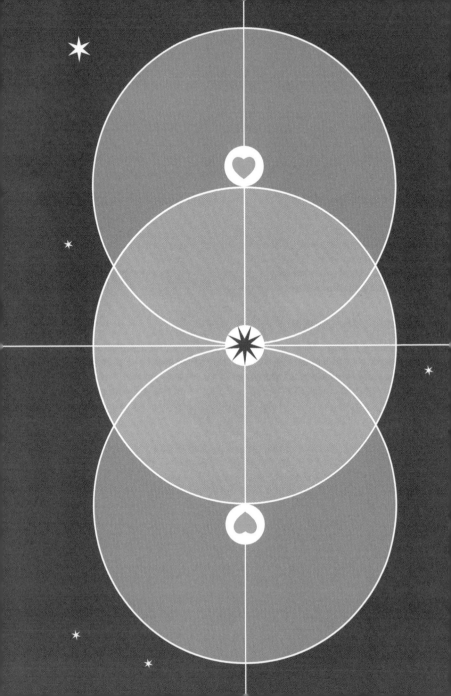

Part two

Your Astrological Toolkit

If you want to get the most out of the rest of this book, it's best to have a basic understanding of astrology so you can see how everything fits together. This section gives you the necessary information by introducing you to some essential astrological building blocks: the twelve signs, the ten planets, the four elements and the three modes. Learning what they all mean and how they connect will give you a deeper insight into the mysteries of Venus and Mars in your own birth chart as well as the charts of some of the people in your life. You'll also discover what it means when Venus and Mars turn retrograde.

✳ The signs and the planets

If you are new to astrology, this section will be essential reading so you can fully understand how to work with Mars and Venus. However, if you already have some knowledge of astrology you can still benefit from refreshing your insight into the behaviour and needs of Venus and Mars in your own life and those of the people around you, whether that's a partner, child, colleague or best friend.

Each of the planets and each zodiac sign is identified by a glyph or symbol. You are probably already familiar with many of them, including Venus's mirror – ♀ – and Mars's spear – ♂. They are frequently used as the symbols for female and male (and, interestingly, the Mars glyph is an old symbol for iron in alchemy, the metal ruled by Mars!). If you familiarize yourself with the symbols, it will make it easier to work with your birth chart.

The following table tells you which planet rules which sign of the zodiac. Originally, when astrologers were only aware of seven planets (in astrology, the Sun and Moon are called planets, even though astrologers know that they are a star and a satellite respectively), five of them were given rulership of two signs each. When Uranus, Neptune and Pluto were discovered, they were added to the list of planetary rulers, so now Scorpio, Aquarius and Pisces have a traditional ruler as well as a modern ruler.

Sign		Traditional ruler		Modern ruler	
♈	Aries	♂	Mars	-	
♉	Taurus	♀	Venus	-	
♊	Gemini	☿	Mercury	-	
♋	Cancer	☽	Moon	-	
♌	Leo	☉	Sun	-	
♍	Virgo	☿	Mercury	-	
♎	Libra	♀	Venus	-	
♏	Scorpio	♂	Mars	♇	Pluto
♐	Sagittarius	♃	Jupiter	-	
♑	Capricorn	♄	Saturn	-	
♒	Aquarius	♄	Saturn	♅	Uranus
♓	Pisces	♃	Jupiter	♆	Neptune

If you refer to this chart you will be able to see whether your Venus and Mars are connected by planetary rulership, even if they don't seem to have much else in common. You can also use it when comparing other people's Venus and Mars positions with yours. Let's say you have Venus in Sagittarius and your partner's Venus is in Pisces. They don't seem to have anything in common, yet when you consult this chart you'll see that your Venus is ruled by Jupiter, which is also the traditional ruler of Pisces, so they share a Jupiter quality. Consult the list of planetary keywords below to see how this Jupiter effect can work.

How the planets affect us

Here are some of the main areas ruled by each of the ten planets. They will help to build up your astrological knowledge by showing you the areas of life that each planet describes.

☉ Sun

Where and how you shine; sense of self; ego; creativity; health; journey through life; leadership; father figures

☽ Moon

What you find familiar and reassuring; habits; home; family; needs; what feeds you; mother figures

☿ Mercury

What you think and talk about; communication skills; youth; versatility; buying and selling; siblings

♀ Venus

What and who you love; enjoyment; pleasure; emotional needs; values; money; ability to give and receive love

♂ Mars

What motivates you; drive; determination; energy; your wants, urges and desires; anger; aggression

♃ Jupiter

Where you grow and expand; wisdom; philosophy; beliefs; travel; optimism; confidence; larger than life

♄ Saturn

What disciplines and restricts you; rules; fears; limitations; boundaries; structures; foundations; authority figures; conventions

♅ Uranus

Where and how you're unique; rebellion; the shock of the new; humanitarianism; being unconventional; originality

♆ Neptune

Where and how you merge with the world; spirituality; the unconscious; search for meaning; romance; imagination; lack of boundaries

♇ Pluto

Where and how you're transformed; intensity; change; survival; elimination; the underworld; what is hidden or taboo

The twelve zodiac signs

There is so much to say about the meaning of each of the twelve signs of the zodiac that entire libraries have been written on the subject. Here, we are only going to consider some of the main characteristics for each sign. Start by looking up the keywords for your Sun sign and play with them in your imagination. Expand on their meanings, consider how they apply to you and start to bring your own birth chart to life.

♈ Aries

Enthusiastic; dynamic; impetuous; impatient; initiative; pioneering; focused on the self

♉ Taurus

Stable; grounded; practical; steady; steadfast; possessive; stubborn; laid back; focused on the material

♊ Gemini

Versatile; changeable; quicksilver; busy; curiosity; low boredom threshold; focused on communication

♋ Cancer

Emotional; moody; intuitive; sensitive; tenacious; defensive; protective; focused on what is familiar

♌ Leo

Creative; warm-hearted; loving; dramatic; loyal; self-expression; pride; dignified; bossy; focused on self-expression

♍ Virgo

Modest; pragmatic; diligent; neat; precise; meticulous; interested in details; analytical; focused on being of service

♎ Libra

Need for balance; courteous; wants harmony; indecisive; diplomatic; focused on relationships

♏ Scorpio

Intense emotions; taboos; secrets; willpower; control; jealousy; inward-looking; focused on transformation

♐ Sagittarius

Outward-looking; expansive; idealistic; optimistic; knowledge; tactless; exaggeration; focused on exploration

♑ Capricorn

Disciplined; rigorous; wisdom; ambition; recognition; respectability; focused on achievement

♒ Aquarius

Original; independent; humanitarian; emotionally detached; rational; dogmatic; focused on ideas

♓ Pisces

Sensitive; instinctive; kind; altruistic; vulnerable; impressionable; escapist; idealistic; focused on compassion

How closely do you match the concepts of your Sun sign in your emotional relationships? As we introduce Mars and Venus and other parts of your chart, you will begin to make more subtle assessments of your astrological influences.

The elements and the modes

In astrology we have ten planets, twelve signs of the zodiac and twelve houses in the birth chart (which we will be discussing later). We also have four elements and three modes, and if you multiply four by three you get twelve. This means that every sign of the zodiac has a unique combination of element and mode, giving it an extra dimension and expression.

Which element are you?

Western astrologers believe that nature is composed of four elements – fire, earth, air and water. They all have a particular way of behaving and reacting, according to the nature of the element involved. For instance, the fire element is warm, enthusiastic and loving. Each element rules three signs, giving its qualities to that sign.

There are four elements, each of which rules three zodiac signs.

Fire

Aries, Leo, Sagittarius

Enthusiastic, warm-hearted, impulsive, outgoing, idealistic

Air

Gemini, Libra, Aquarius

Intelligent, communicative, interested in ideas

Earth

Taurus, Virgo, Capricorn

Grounded, stable, practical, dependable, obstinate

Water

Cancer, Scorpio, Pisces

Emotional, sensitive, empathic, caring

Which mode are you?

The three modes are known as cardinal, fixed and mutable.
They describe our attitude and approach to life, and each
one rules four signs.

Cardinal

Aries,
Cancer, Libra,
Capricorn

Determined,
motivated,
ambitious, tenacious

Fixed

Taurus, Leo,
Scorpio,
Aquarius

Focused, stubborn,
emphatic, resistant
to change

Mutable

Gemini, Virgo,
Sagittarius,
Pisces

Fluid, changeable,
versatile, needs
room to manoeuvre

Relating the element and modes

Every planet in your birth chart belongs to a sign that has a particular element and mode. You can look up the element and mode of your Sun sign to increase your perception of it, and then move on to the elements and modes of your Venus and Mars signs. You can have great insights when you play with the images that are conjured up by combining an element and mode. Fixed water is ice, so how do you translate that into your understanding of Scorpio? Perhaps it's emotion that is held tightly but can melt in the right circumstances. Cardinal fire burns hard and fast, which sounds exactly like Aries. Sometimes it can get out of control, just as Aries can sometimes be too impetuous. The elements and modes that rule your Venus and Mars will affect your relationships because they influence the way you react to other people and the type of relationships you're looking for.

Looking at the elements of someone else's Venus or Mars is also very useful, as is combining their Venus element with your Mars element, and vice versa. Fire and air signs get on well together (air feeds fire), as do earth and water signs (water moves earth). However, elements that sit next to each other in the table below, such as fire and earth (earth puts out fire), are not so compatible.

	Fire	Earth	Air	Water
Cardinal	Aries	Capricorn	Libra	Cancer
Fixed	Leo	Taurus	Aquarius	Scorpio
Mutable	Sagittarius	Virgo	Gemini	Pisces

How to find your Venus and Mars positions

Discovering the positions that Venus and Mars occupied at the time of your birth opens up a wealth of information about the inner you, especially where your relationships are concerned. This knowledge, which you can explore in detail in this book, will answer all sorts of questions about yourself and also shed light on hitherto hidden areas of your character and the way you relate to others.

Your Venus sign reveals some of the most sensitive and delicate areas of your personality, as well as what you yearn for emotionally and the way you show love, while your Mars sign shows how you are able to assert yourself with others and the things that you want from life – and from your relationships, because Mars is the planet of desire, motivation and your sexual urges.

If you don't already know which zodiac signs your Venus and Mars occupied when you were born, all you need to do is consult the charts at the back this book, armed with the following information:

The date of your birth	The time of your birth	The place of your birth
	which may help you to fine-tune your Venus or Mars sign if it moved signs on the day in question	if you need to do that fine-tuning

Even if you're longing to know about the chart of your beloved or your children, it's a good idea to begin with your own chart. It's highly likely that you know yourself better than you know anyone else, so you can apply what you read here about your Venus and Mars signs to what you know about yourself. Be patient and don't try to rush through the process, especially if you're completely new to the idea of exploring your own birth chart.

Here's what to do, step by step. If your birth year doesn't appear in the tables, turn to page 175 to find out where to go for more help.

Step one

Look up your date of birth in the Venus tables at the back of the book. Look for the nearest date before your birth date and the nearest date after your birth date. This will tell you which sign Venus occupied on the day of your birth. For instance, if you were born on 15 September 1987, you will see that Venus entered Virgo on 23 August and moved into Libra on 16 September, so your Venus is in Virgo.

If you were born on the day the signs changed, you will need to do some more investigation in Step three.

Step two

Now do the same with the position of Mars on the day of your birth. If you look at the Mars tables, you'll see that Mars entered Virgo on 22 August and stayed there until 8 October, so you were born with Mars in Virgo.

Every so often Venus or Mars will turn retrograde (backwards, from our perspective on Earth, see page 40) and may even move into the previous sign. If this happens, you will see it marked clearly in the tables with 'R' for 'retrograde'. When the planet turns direct or forwards again, that motion is shown with 'D' for 'direct'.

As before, if you were born on the day the signs change, go to Step three.

Step three

If you were born within a few hours of a planet changing signs (and up to 12 hours if you were born far from the UK, for reasons about to be explained), you need to know the time of your birth in order to discover which sign the planet was in when you were born.

In astrology, we always use Universal Time (UT), also known as Greenwich Mean Time (GMT) because all the world's time zones begin at Greenwich, in London. So, wherever you were born, you need to convert the time to UT in order to use the tables.

The easiest way to do this with your own chart is to use an online computer astrology program (see page 175). If you enter your date, place and time of birth, the program will do all the calculations for you and give you the exact degree and sign of every planet in your chart, including Venus and Mars. Even if you were born in the UK during the winter, when UT is usually in operation, you may find that British Summer Time (BST) was being used.

Step four

If you aren't sure of your time of birth, try to make a guess based on any information you have, such as 'it was around teatime'. If you have no idea at all, choose noon because this is the midpoint of the day.

Step five

Read up about the relevant sign. Does it sound like you? If it doesn't, read the other possible sign. Does that sound better? Some books state that if you were born with a planet on the cusp of two signs, that planet has a bit of both signs in its nature, but this isn't true. That planet is in one sign or the other, not a combination of the two!

Step six

If you have an accurate time of birth and have used an astrology program to calculate your birth chart, you will not only know the signs of Venus and Mars but also the houses they occupy in your chart. You can read up about Venus in the houses on pages 70–73 and Mars in the houses on pages 102–105.

Step seven

You can use the Venus and Mars tables in other ways, too. Want to know more about a big emotional moment in your life? Look up the date in the tables! You can also find the current signs of both planets, and then refer to the relevant sections of the book to learn how those signs are affecting you and your relationships right now.

Ready to move on

If you take this a step at a time, you will find it is a lot easier than it sounds. Now you're ready to make the most of this book. Read up about yourself first, and then you can investigate the emotional make-up of your nearest and dearest. You could discover all sorts of ways to improve your understanding of them, and therefore how to get on better with the people in your life.

✳✳ Relating
✳✳ with Venus
✳✳ and Mars

If your previous experience of astrology focused primarily on your Sun sign – the sign occupied by the Sun when you were born – you're about to take your astrological knowledge to the next level. With the Sun, you're concentrating on the single combination of the Sun and the relevant zodiac sign, but with Venus and Mars, of course, you're looking at two planets and possibly two signs. And that's when things can become slightly more complicated because there are more astrological combinations to consider.

So before you look deeper into your Venus and Mars signs, you need to understand what they represent astrologically. Venus is all about love, enjoyment, affection, the need for harmony and what makes us happy, while Mars describes our drives, motivations and urges, as well as our sexual needs and what gets us fired up, whether with enthusiasm or anger.

This means that the way you express love through your Venus sign may not tie in with the way you express your sexual desires through your Mars sign. Your Venus and Mars may even have entirely different ways of handling relationships.

When we contradict ourselves

Most of us are well aware of our internal contradictions, especially if they're pointed out by loved ones during what politicians like to call 'a free and frank exchange of views'. These contradictions are spelt out in great detail in our birth charts, as you'll have discovered for yourself if you've ever explored your own chart. These personality clashes within us can make life very interesting. Walt Whitman summed up our own internal contradictions perfectly in his poem *Song of Myself, 51*.

Do I contradict myself?
Very well then I contradict myself,
(I am large, I contain multitudes.)

Now you have established the positions of Venus and Mars in your chart, you may find that their signs are telling different stories about you, too. This means that your approach to relationships, which are so strongly influenced by Venus and Mars, could also be full of contradictions. If this applies to you, let me reassure you that there are no right or wrong combinations in astrology. Having an incompatible Venus and Mars doesn't mean that you're hopeless at dealing with others, it simply means that the way you express love is very different from the way you express your sexual needs.

Some people are born with several planets congregating in one or two signs, while others have planets scattered all around their charts, so birth charts don't all look the same, and if your Venus and Mars are in different signs it doesn't mean that you've made a mistake in looking them up, although it's always wise to double-check just in case.

Are your Venus and Mars talking to each other?

When you've discovered the signs occupied by your Venus and Mars, you need to work out whether they are speaking the same astrological language. Do they understand each other? Do they share the same relationship goals? Alternatively, are they so different that they might as well be speaking gobbledegook to one another, in which case you need to act as their interpreter?

It all depends on the signs they occupy and whether they have a connection with one another, such as being in the same or a complementary element or mode. They can be connected by either an element or a mode, but are only connected by both if they're in the same sign. Sometimes, the signs aren't linked by element or mode, so appear to have nothing in common at all. If so, check to see if they have the same planetary rulers (see pages 22–25).

Even if you can't refer to your birth chart, simply knowing the relationship by sign between your Venus and Mars will give you important background information about the way they connect.

Relative positions of Venus and Mars

If you do have a copy of your birth chart, you can see whether your Venus and Mars are within a certain number of degrees of one another – this is known as being in aspect. Each aspect has an allowable orb of a specific number of degrees either side of it, as you will see. Here are the six most significant aspects.

☌ Conjunction

Both planets are in the same sign; allow an orb of 8°

△ Trine

Separated by 120°; allow an orb of 6°

✳ Sextile

Separated by one sign, so by 60°; allow an orb of 4°

⚲ Inconjunct or quincunx

Separated by 150°; allow an orb of 2°

□ Square

Separated by 90°; allow an orb of 6°

☍ Opposition

Separated by 180°; allow an orb of 8°

Even if you don't know your birth chart, you can work out the number of signs that separate your Venus and Mars. Start with the planet that comes earliest in the zodiac (bearing in mind that they move around the chart in an anticlockwise direction) and then count round until you get to the second planet. For instance, if you have Venus in Sagittarius and Mars in Taurus, you start with Mars and then count round until you get to Venus.

The information below doesn't only apply to your own Venus and Mars. You can use it to discover how your Venus connects with someone else's Mars, and vice versa.

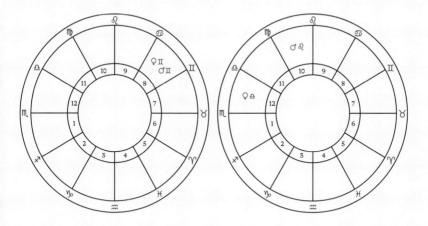

Conjunction by sign

This is when both planets occupy the same sign, such as Venus in Gemini and Mars in Gemini. In this case, your Venus style of loving is expressed in the same way as your Mars style of sex and motivation. This can be good news because the two planets understand each other, but it can also mean that you are so accustomed to behave in the style of that sign in relationships that it doesn't even occur to you to do things differently.

Take note of the element and mode of the relevant sign because this will give you further information about the way your Venus and Mars operate.

Sextile by sign

Here, the planets are separated by one entire sign, for example Venus in Libra and Mars in Leo, separated by Virgo. This puts them in complementary elements: either fire and air or earth and water. Each has its own style of expression but they are compatible with one another.

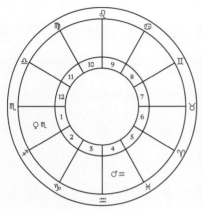 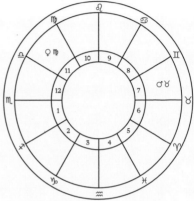

Square by sign

Venus and Mars are separated by two entire signs. Here Venus is in Scorpio and Mars in Aquarius, so they are separated by Sagittarius and Capricorn. Signs in square aspect are therefore in the same mode: cardinal, fixed or water. They have different styles of expression but they share the same basic attitude to relationships.

Trine by sign

In a trine, the planets are separated by three entire signs. In this example Venus in Virgo and Mars in Taurus are divided by Gemini, Cancer and Leo. Planets in trine share the same element – in this case Earth – and therefore have a similar style of behaviour.

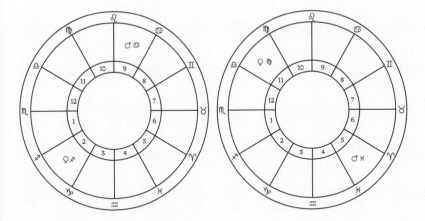

Inconjunct by sign

Here, four entire signs – Leo, Virgo, Libra and Scorpio – separate Venus in Sagittarius and Mars in Cancer, and share neither element nor mode. They apparently don't understand one another at all when inconjunct by sign, so the way you express your Venus is at odds with your Mars. The two planets want different things from relationships and you must find some middle ground, or at the very least be aware of your conflicting emotional and sexual urges so you can deal with them consciously.

Two of the inconjunct sign pairings are ruled by the same planet, giving them something in common after all. These are Taurus and Libra (both ruled by Venus) and Aries and Scorpio (Mars rules Aries and is the traditional ruler of Scorpio).

Opposition by sign

The planets are separated by five entire signs. Here, Venus in Virgo and Mars in Pisces are split by Libra, Scorpio, Sagittarius, Capricorn and Aquarius. Planets in opposition share the same mode. They are complete opposites yet they are connected because they sit at each end of the same axis. Think of this axis as the planetary version of a see-saw. You want to keep both ends balanced, so you need to express both signs equally rather than focusing on one to the detriment of the other.

Going retrograde – but don't panic!

Every planet in the solar system, other than the Sun and Moon, turns retrograde at some point in its cycle and appears to move backwards through the heavens. Venus and Mars are no exception, but what does it mean when they turn retrograde? Does it cause emotional disaster?

Before we get on to how a retrograde Venus or Mars can affect us, let's look at what happens astronomically. Retrograde means that from the Earth a planet appears to be travelling backwards through the sky. Of course, planets don't really move backwards, it is an illusion caused by the fact that the planets orbit the Sun at different speeds and distances. When the Earth passes a slower-moving outer planet, that planet appears to move backwards. The planet seems to slow down and then stop completely. This is called 'stationing'. The planet then turns retrograde for a while, before stationing again and then moving forwards, which is known as 'going direct'. In the Venus and Mars tables at the back of the book you'll see that these phases are marked with 'R' and 'D'. The planet will either stay in the same sign while it moves retrograde (R) or go back into the previous sign before going direct (D) again.

Retrograde planets affect us in two different ways – when the planets are retrograde at the time of birth (natal retrogrades) and when they go retrograde by transit (when they are moving across the sky).

Natal retrogrades

The way to understand how your retrograde planet affects you is to think of it as going against the tide. So your way of expressing that planet in that sign is different from that of someone born when that planet was in direct motion in that sign. A retrograde natal Venus can display love differently from the way you'd expect from that sign: you might feel shy or hesitant about showing your affection (Venus retrograde in Leo); you may have problems with your family (Venus retrograde in Cancer); or you might not care about material values (Venus retrograde in Taurus). A retrograde natal Mars could assert itself in an unusual way (Mars retrograde in Aries); you might be reticent about getting involved sexually (Mars retrograde in Scorpio); or you may work extra hard to achieve your goals (Mars retrograde in Capricorn).

Transiting retrogrades

Put simply, a transit is the course that a planet takes as it travels across the sky. Right this minute, as you're reading this, all the planets are transiting across the solar system and maybe Venus or Mars has gone retrograde. How would this affect you? Look on it as an opportunity to reconsider and reflect on the meaning of that planet in that sign. For instance, retrograde Venus in Gemini could be a time to review the way you communicate with some of the people in your life. Retrograde Mars in Cancer could be when you put those plans to renovate your home on hold or when you realize that they need to be rethought. You should also try to avoid starting a new project relating to the sign in question when Mars is retrograde, and avoid making a big emotional or financial commitment when Venus is retrograde.

If you have a copy of your birth chart you can see which house is being transited by the retrograde planet, which gives you further clues about how it might affect you. And don't forget that you can look back at previous retrogrades to see whether they were significant for you. It's a great way to learn how your own chart works and which areas of it are particularly sensitive.

Part three

The Astrology of Venus

In this section of the book you'll discover how Venus affects your relationships, whatever their nature. Your connection with a romantic partner, your links with your family, your friendships and your working relationships are all coloured and influenced by the sign that Venus occupied when you were born. Venus is never more than 47° from the Sun, meaning that your Venus sign will be the same sign as your Sun, or in one of the two signs before the Sun or one of the two signs that follow it. After reading about your own Venus sign, and how it behaves in combination with your Sun sign, you can learn about the role that Venus plays in the charts of your nearest and dearest. If you have an accurate birth time and natal chart, you can also discover what Venus's house position says about the area of life where you naturally express your Venusian energies.

What Venus represents in astrology

Affection, attraction, enjoyment, happiness – these are all part of Venus's realm because this is the planet that rules the pleasure principle. Venus governs what makes us happy in life as well as in love. Whenever you do something that brings you joy or puts a huge smile on your face, you are expressing the sign, house position or aspects of Venus in your birth chart. There are many combinations of the position of Venus in your chart, but remember that Venus will always be in your own Sun sign or one of the two signs before or after.

Above all, Venus rules love. When we talk about love, many of us immediately think of relationships. But Venus also tells us about the things and activities we love. The sign occupied by Venus in your birth chart describes what – and who – you love, as well as the way you love it. For instance, if you have Venus in Aries you will show love in the quick, impetuous way that is so characteristic of Aries. If you fall for someone, you don't want to wait until a week on Wednesday before declaring undying love. You want to do it right now, while you're in the mood. Also, the person you love will show some Arian qualities. You will enjoy activities governed by Aries or that carry the flavour of Mars, which is the planetary ruler of Aries.

Giving it meaning

Venus has a lot to say about our values, too. These are the areas of life that really matter to us, whether they're people, relationships, activities, principles, ideas or possessions. They are what we're prepared to invest our time or money in because we consider them to be worthwhile and because they enhance our lives in some way. Other planets in our birth chart can also influence what we value, but Venus is a major player.

The charm game

Venus is one of the planets that rules charm, with Neptune being the other one. Venus likes life to be pleasant, easy-going, relaxed and enjoyable, and one way to achieve this is to be as charming as possible. It reduces the likelihood of someone getting angry or creating an unpleasant atmosphere – two things that Venus finds difficult to manage. People with a strong Venus in their chart, such as Venus in its own signs of Taurus or Libra, or Venus conjunct the Sun, have a wonderful ability to tune into others at an emotional level and instinctively know how to put them at their ease by saying or doing the right things. These are the people who can diffuse someone's anger in a trice with a few carefully chosen words and a sweet smile.

As sweet as sugar

'Sweet' is a very Venusian word. Venus knows how to be sweet to someone. However, anyone expressing this Venusian sweetness must guard against overdoing it and coming across as a little too sugary for comfort or, worse still, insincere. So, ideally, Venus should concentrate on the charm and avoid the smarm.

Natal Venus in Aries

What does it mean to be born with Venus in Aries? You're about to find out, whether you're reading about yourself or someone else. Planets don't work in isolation, so in this section you'll discover the sort of team that's made by your Venus and Sun signs.

Element	Mode	Keywords
Fire	Cardinal	Impulsive, fun-loving, direct

Enthusiastic, assertive, lively and dynamic, there's no way anyone could ignore you. Well, not for long, anyway, because you'll soon make your presence felt. Venus rules the things we love, and you absolutely adore being noticed and appreciated. You can't bear the thought of being overlooked and will soon get ratty if you're left on the sidelines for too long. Let's face it, you can't resist being the centre of attention. You can thank the sign of Aries for this, but you need to make sure this need for attention doesn't spill over into being completely self-centred and only interested in what matters to you.

One of your greatest charms is your generosity towards the people you love. You enjoy giving them little treats and buying them gifts on the spur of the moment, simply to show your appreciation or because you know they'll love what you've got them.

Venus is a planet that needs to create harmony, but that isn't always easy when it's in Aries because this is a sign that can't help seeing red every now and then. If you have other planets in Aries, or a strong Mars, you might even think that there's nothing like a good row. You can really let rip, throw a few things around in the heat of the moment and get several grievances off your chest, and then you can have a wonderful time kissing and making up. For you, an argument flares up quickly and subsides just as fast, and then it's all forgotten. Whether other people are as happy to forgive and forget is another matter, of course.

Sun in Aquarius,
Venus in Aries

Freedom-loving; independent; strong-willed;
a need to do things your own way; a love of the new;
sensitive and idealistic.

Sun in Pisces,
Venus in Aries

Emotional; compassionate but can be feisty;
generous; loving and affectionate; easily hurt when
let down or betrayed.

Sun in Aries,
Venus in Aries

Energetic, enthusiastic; you love to get the most
out of every day; you quickly bounce back after
disappointments and setbacks; you can't bear
being ignored.

Sun in Taurus,
Venus in Aries

Slow Taurean practicality clashes with Aries
impatience; loyal and loving but can be bored;
a lively and entertaining partner is a must.

Sun in Gemini,
Venus in Aries

Dynamic, energetic; you enjoy life when it's busy
but get bored when things slow down; flirty and
fun-loving; not always completely faithful.

Natal Venus in Taurus

To be born with Venus in Taurus is a fascinating combination and you'll find out why in this section, whether you want to know about yourself or someone else. Here you'll discover how your Venus and Sun signs work together, as planets never work in isolation.

Element	Mode	Keywords
Earth	Fixed	Sensual, loving, security-conscious

Venus rules Taurus (and also Libra), so being born with this placing means you have a double dose of Venusian energy. You're affectionate and easy-going, and do your best to get along with the people around you. Very often you simply can't be bothered to get in a stew about something because it's too much effort, so you'd rather ignore it. However, on the rare occasions that you do get angry, everyone will know about it. Think of a normally placid bull that's finally been goaded once too often!

Venus is all about pleasure, and when it's in Taurus it means that you enjoy the simple things in life. That could be a barefoot walk through the grass with your beloved, a glass of deliciously chilled white wine while watching the sun set or dipping into your secret stash of chocolate whenever you feel a bit low. Food is one of your great pleasures, especially if you can share it with others. It's also a wonderful form of comfort whenever the going gets tough, even if this can have an unfortunate impact on your weight and make you suspect that all your clothes have shrunk in the wardrobe. You love the sensual aspect of food, too – its taste, its texture and colour.

You love having people around you but you must feel that you can trust them. Being so loyal and faithful yourself, you expect nothing less from the people you love and will be bitterly hurt if they ever let you down.

Sun in Pisces,
Venus in Taurus

Life must be gentle; you combine Piscean compassion
with Taurean need to give practical help; romantic,
sensuous and loving.

Sun in Aries,
Venus in Taurus

Energetic and enterprising; you enjoy succeeding in life
and rising to challenges; your emotions are never far
from the surface; relationships must involve passion.

Sun in Taurus,
Venus in Taurus

You like to take things slowly; strong need for
enjoyment and sensual gratification; ability to relax
can come across as laziness; tactile.

Sun in Gemini,
Venus in Taurus

Meeting interesting people is enjoyable but you
are happiest when connecting at a deep level;
easy-going Gemini attitude to relationships
clashes with Taurean possessiveness.

Sun in Cancer,
Venus in Taurus

Continually searching for emotional comfort
and security; you prefer to avoid difficult situations
and unpleasant people; a happy home and family life
are essential.

Natal Venus in Gemini

Here you can find out what it means to be born with Venus in Gemini – whether you're finding out about yourself or a loved one. Planets don't work alone, so here you'll learn what kind of team is made by your Venus and Sun signs.

Element	Mode	Keywords
Air	Mutable	Adaptable, charming, social butterfly

You probably have a long string of admirers who are drawn to your poise, sparkling conversation and youthful appearance. And long may that last! As you get older your looks and general attitude will belie your age, so you give the impression of being much younger than you really are. Venus in Gemini gives you a lightness of touch when communicating with other people, so you have no problems in finding the right thing to say in even the stickiest moments. Your tact and clever way with words come in handy in every area of your life, although you must guard against a tendency to say what you think people want to hear rather than telling them the truth, especially if you're trying to wriggle out of a tight spot.

Having Venus in Gemini means you enjoy a wide range of activities, particularly if they involve reading, writing, chatting or playing. For instance, children love you, thanks to your willingness to lark about with them, play silly games or give them lots of treats. You love keeping on the move, so you need plenty of changes of scene. Being stuck in one place for too long can make you very jaded and stale, and being with the same people, day in and day out, can feel equally tedious. Variety is definitely the spice of life as far as you're concerned, to ensure that you never run the awful risk of getting bored.

Sun in Aries,
Venus in Gemini

Lively, energetic and game for almost anything; life feels like an adventure; emotional relationships must be easy-going and light-hearted.

Sun in Taurus,
Venus in Gemini

Placid Taurus combines with Gemini pep and vivacity; not as possessive as other Taureans but you may not have their rock-solid fidelity either.

Sun in Gemini,
Venus in Gemini

Playful, flirtatious, lively and terrific fun to be around; forever youthful, with a Peter Pan quality; can't bear melodramatic or over-emotional scenes.

Sun in Cancer,
Venus in Gemini

You look after loved ones and keep them entertained; lots of energy goes into family and home life; you need interests away from home, too.

Sun in Leo,
Venus in Gemini

Dazzling, attractive and charming; the classic Leo warmth, protectiveness and strong emotions but with a light touch.

Natal Venus in Cancer

With your Venus in Cancer at the time you were born, you are likely to demonstrate a particular way of dealing with relationships – and here you can discover why. Whether you are finding out about your partner, friend or relation, or thinking about yourself, you'll discover that planets don't work in isolation, and what kind of team your Venus and Sun signs are likely to make.

Element	Mode	Keywords
Water	Cardinal	Warm, protective, moody

This placing is all about your emotions. Just like the sea, they ebb and flow, and in times of difficulty it's almost impossible for you to get them into any kind of balance. This means that you can be very moody, with everyone around you left in no doubt about the way you're feeling, whether that's up or down. When times are good, you ooze warmth, love and a very maternal quality, so loved ones know that you care about them. When times are hard, you can shut down and put up a defensive barrier that's hard to penetrate, simply as a way of protecting your very vulnerable emotions.

Having a sense of family is essential to you, although it may not be a conventional family unit. Instead, it could be the family you've created from a close gang of friends or the animals you look after. Whatever its nature, it gives you the all-important emotional security that you crave so much. Home is a vital part of your life because it offers you a solid base and a place of retreat. Finances permitting (and you will happily save up the money if you can), you like the idea of owning your own property and may even have been the first of your friends to buy a flat or house. At its best, home is your refuge from the turbulent world, and you enjoy making it as cosy and welcoming as possible. Ideally, you need to share it with someone or something, such as a pet or even some houseplants, because it's vital that you have an outlet for your need to take care of others.

Sun in Taurus,
Venus in Cancer

You crave physical and emotional security; a stable and comfortable home base is crucial, preferably shared with some cherished companions.

Sun in Gemini,
Venus in Cancer

Hidden emotional depths combine with great warmth; a magpie who enjoys collecting all sorts of things, including people.

Sun in Cancer,
Venus in Cancer

You wear your heart on your sleeve; you need to be needed and to have people to love but must give them room to breathe; a cosy home is a must.

Sun in Leo,
Venus in Cancer

Warm and demonstrative; you have a talent for taking care of people although that may also involve being bossy; you need a safe refuge from the world.

Sun in Virgo,
Venus in Cancer

Must balance a tendency to be analytical with a need to express emotions; will only reveal deeper feelings when it seems safe to do so.

Natal Venus in Leo

Those with Venus in Leo – or wanting to find out about someone else with that configuration in their chart – will discover here what they need to know. Remember that planets work together and this will give you some insight into the Venus and Sun-sign team in your chart.

Element	Mode	Keywords
Fire	Fixed	Loving, proud, creative

You have a deep need to be noticed and appreciated by the rest of the world, otherwise you start to feel ignored – and that's something you really can't bear. Leo is a very showy sign, so your Venus has an innate desire to stand out from the crowd. This is the classic placing for someone who enjoys performing in some way, especially if it's on stage, because you soak up the applause like a thirsty sponge. You might be the lynchpin of the local theatre group, or maybe you're aiming higher than that. After all, Leo is a sign that doesn't do things by halves because, quite frankly, it would be demeaning to appear as anything less than your absolute best.

Any interests that allow you to express your true self are ideal, and there is plenty to choose from thanks to your natural gift for creative and artistic activities. Find something that you excel at, so that you can enjoy every minute of it. One area of expertise that's instinctive is showing love and affection to the important people in your life. Regardless of your Sun sign, you need to be able to express your emotions in whichever way seems most appropriate at the time. Family life means a lot to you, and if you're a parent you'll be very proud of your offspring, but you'll also expect them to earn that pride. You'll make your feelings very plain if you think that your children are slacking or showing you up in some way. You also need to be able to feel proud of your partner. After all, you have an image to maintain!

Sun in Gemini,
Venus in Leo

Witty, entertaining and terrific company; you fizz with
ideas and enthusiasm; can be the centre of attention;
a great gift for friendship and can be very loyal.

Sun in Cancer,
Venus in Leo

A slightly reserved persona, but much more openly
affectionate with people who are trusted; needs to
have a strong sense of belonging.

Sun in Leo,
Venus in Leo

Dramatic, passionate and impossible to ignore; can be
playful and carefree, but you never completely lose
your innate dignity.

Sun in Virgo,
Venus in Leo

Modest and precise on the surface but more relaxed
and fun-loving in private; you must unwind every now
and then; you take pride in doing things well.

Sun in Libra,
Venus in Leo

Love and romance are guiding lights; a magnet for
admiring friends, family and lovers; idealism can lead
to a broken heart but hope springs eternal.

Natal Venus in Virgo

This section will help those with Venus in Virgo, or those looking to understand someone else with that pairing, find out about how they express their love and deal with relationships. Read on to discover how the planetary team of Venus and your Sun sign work together.

Element	Mode	Keywords
Earth	Mutable	Modest, shy, cautious

You take a careful approach to love. Maybe you don't entirely trust a new relationship to work out well or prefer to look before you leap into making a commitment. Whatever your reasons, you are discriminating about the people you get involved with and expect them to fulfil certain criteria. Virgo is the sign of hygiene and cleanliness, so you want everyone in your life to maintain decent standards. Anyone who's a stranger to soap and hot water will soon be a stranger to you because you'll go out of your way to avoid them.

Whatever your Sun sign, you like creating order out of chaos. It gives you a sense of purpose and also the feeling that you're in charge of your life, even if it's in a modest way. 'Modest' is one of the adjectives that best describes your approach to emotions and 'shy' is another. You aren't keen on making a big fuss, even if you feel something very strongly, and major displays of temperament from others make you cringe with embarrassment. How can anyone show themselves up like that? Creating and maintaining a reputation for being polite and well-behaved is important to you, even if you reveal a surprisingly raunchy side in private. You're careful with money, too, because you don't want to squander it – you never know when you might need to draw on that nest-egg you've stashed away so carefully for a rainy day.

Sun in Cancer,
Venus in Virgo

Emotionally reserved; a need to help others;
houseproud; enjoys being of service; prudent
approach to finances.

Sun in Leo,
Venus in Virgo

The Leo flair is tempered by Virgo reticence; a good
and faithful friend; you enjoy taking care of yourself.

Sun in Virgo,
Venus in Virgo

An emphasis on modesty and shyness; a love of doing
things properly; perfectionist with high standards.

Sun in Libra,
Venus in Virgo

Intelligent and considerate; charming and polite, and
keen to create a good impression; analytical.

Sun in Scorpio,
Venus in Virgo

The profound Scorpio energy is held in check by Virgo;
you enjoy showing great passion with the right person.

Natal Venus in Libra

If you have worked out that you – or someone you know – has Venus in Libra, here is where you read about the characteristics of anyone with that configuration in their chart. Remember that planets work together and this will give you some insight into the Venus and Sun-sign team in your chart.

Element	Mode	Keywords
Air	Cardinal	Elegant, diplomatic, considerate

Libra is one of the two signs ruled by Venus (Taurus being the other), so Venus is very much at home here. You've been given more than your fair share of tact and charm, which means you're renowned for your ability to get on well with almost everyone you meet. Even if you can't stand them, they'll never know. You really dislike rocking the boat or getting embroiled in arguments, so will sometimes adopt the policy of peace at any price simply because life is so much easier that way. Unfortunately, if you do this for too long, you run the risk of giving others the impression that they can continue to call the shots, which is when putting yourself second and others first will start to frustrate you. You'll finally snap, which can then lead to the very disagreements you were hoping to avoid. Libra is famously indecisive and having Venus in Libra can make you prefer to say what you think others want to hear in order to please them. You probably know exactly what you'd like to say, if only you didn't worry about the ructions this might cause, but maybe you should speak up once in a while.

You yearn for life to be as cultured, civilized and enjoyable as possible, and that can work out expensive if you develop a taste for luxury. Roughing it simply isn't your style, so you're far more at home in a five-star hotel or decent restaurant than in a tent pitched on a muddy campsite, trying to cook sausages in the pouring rain. You might try lowering your high standards once, to show willing and be a good sport, but you won't do it twice.

Sun in Leo,
Venus in Libra

Love, laughter and luxury; idealistic; loyal; a need
for togetherness and to be appreciated.

Sun in Virgo,
Venus in Libra

A need for other people and to help them;
perfectionist; a tendency to criticize the ones you love.

Sun in Libra,
Venus in Libra

Romantically inclined; in love with love, which can
lead to disillusionment when reality intrudes.

Sun in Scorpio,
Venus in Libra

Emotional intensity held in check by a desire
to be seen as polite and considerate.

Sun in Sagittarius,
Venus in Libra

Fun-loving and intelligent; instinctive independence
is tempered by the need for togetherness.

Natal Venus in Scorpio

Find out what it means to be born with Venus in Scorpio, whether you are interested in yourself or someone else. Planets don't work in isolation, so in this section you'll discover the sort of team that's made by your Venus and Sun signs.

Element	Mode	Keywords
Water	Fixed	Intense, passionate, powerful

Love is not something to be taken lightly. You're loyal and passionate, and pour your heart and soul into your relationships, expecting the same kind of commitment from the other person. If this fails to materialize for some reason, you feel disheartened and betrayed. You might even decide to turn your back on love completely because you've been so badly hurt. If someone does break your heart, you will struggle to forgive and forget. Even if you do almost forget, you may never quite forgive. This is a placing that's associated with exacting revenge, and you may contemplate getting your own back, even if you never put those plans into action.

Scorpio is an all-or-nothing sign, so having Venus here gives a very dramatic quality to your relationships, especially the ones involving sex or deep emotions. During times of great intensity you struggle to find emotional balance and self-control because everything feels so intense. You're swept away by a storm of turbulent feelings that often take on a life-or-death aspect, so you need a partner who can keep you grounded. Sex is a very big deal for you, whether that's because you like plenty of it or because you've renounced it for ever. Either way, you have strong feelings on the subject. Jealousy is something to guard against because it can rear its ugly head in all sorts of situations and relationships, with the potential to create havoc.

Money is another topic that you take seriously. Some with this placing relish the power that money gives them and the ability to call the tune. Others are generous, willingly sharing their money and possessions with the people they care about.

Sun in Virgo,
Venus in Scorpio

Intense emotional fires beneath a quiet persona;
analytical, thoughtful and questioning.

Sun in Libra,
Venus in Scorpio

A need to balance deep emotions and keep them in
check; considerable charm and personality.

Sun in Scorpio,
Venus in Scorpio

Very powerful, with profound emotional reserves; you
can be carried away by intense passion.

Sun in Sagittarius,
Venus in Scorpio

Your freedom-loving Sun can sit uneasily with your
emotional intensity; loyal and philosophical.

Sun in Capricorn,
Venus in Scorpio

Matters of the heart are serious stuff; you can be scared
of being hurt or rejected; a need to be understood.

Natal Venus in Sagittarius

Here is what it means to be born with Venus in Sagittarius. It applies both to you and anyone else with the same Venus sign. Planets don't work in isolation, so this explains how your Venus and Sun signs work together or against each other.

Element	Mode	Keywords
Fire	Mutable	Enthusiastic, independent, free-wheeling

You're happiest when life feels like one big adventure. You adore the idea of being able to explore new experiences and fresh opportunities, with the exciting sense that you're never quite sure what's around the corner – except that, with luck, it will be fun. With this happy-go-lucky attitude, it's no surprise that people enjoy being with you and feel better for your cheery company. They revel in your sense of humour, your playfulness and your affectionate nature. You sometimes promise more than you can deliver, perhaps because you're full of generous impulses that seem like a good idea at the time but are soon forgotten because you've got something new to think about, but the people in your life are prepared to overlook that because you're such fun to be around.

Sagittarius is the sign of the philosopher and you enjoy dipping your toes into all kinds of philosophies and beliefs. Sometimes you encounter an idea that really grabs your fertile imagination or just feels right, and which becomes a guiding light in your life. Even if you don't have a deep personal belief, you have strong views and convictions that you love to discuss with anyone who'll listen. However, you should stop short at trying to convert others to your particular view of the world and remember that we're all entitled to our own opinions. You're generous with money and enjoy spending it on yourself and loved ones, especially if you're buying books, interesting artefacts or booking up your next voyage of exploration.

Sun in Libra,
Venus in Sagittarius

Charming and courteous; engaging; enthusiastic;
interested in life; intelligent.

Sun in Scorpio,
Venus in Sagittarius

Scorpio intensity enlivened by Sagittarian optimism;
life must have a purpose.

Sun in Sagittarius,
Venus in Sagittarius

Carefree; positive attitude; wholehearted sense
of humour; interested in travel and ideas.

Sun in Capricorn,
Venus in Sagittarius

A blend of pessimism and optimism; a lifelong love
of learning; experience brings wisdom.

Sun in Aquarius,
Venus in Sagittarius

Fascinated by ideas and philosophies; independent;
a free spirit.

Natal Venus in Capricorn

Certain characteristics result from having your Venus in Capricorn and you are about to find out what they are. You can use this information for yourself or someone else to find out how the Sun and Venus work together to make you who you are.

Element	Mode	Keywords
Earth	Cardinal	Composed, reserved, respectable

Love is a serious business for you. You approach it with caution, concerned about being hurt or rejected, and also anxious that it might not work out in the way you want, leading to heartbreak. It's great when someone loves you but you need them to respect you, too. You don't want to be treated like an also-ran or a dogsbody, and you'll make your feelings known in a very no-nonsense and dignified way if you suspect that you are being taken for granted.

Something to beware of, because of its potential to make you unhappy, is a tendency to look on the gloomy side where your relationships are concerned. If a love affair has gone wrong in the past, you might tell yourself that your new relationship will go the same way, even if everything is absolutely marvellous. There can also be difficulties if you're so emotionally reserved that you struggle to express your feelings to others, because your shyness might be mistaken for disinterest. Alternatively, a partner might be astonished the first time they discover that your buttoned-down image is only for the outside world and that you're much less inhibited and possibly even completely outrageous in private.

Very often there's an age gap between you and your beloved, especially if they're the older one. You aren't aware of the difference in age and may even enjoy being looked after by someone who's older or wiser than you. In extreme cases, you may be tempted to get together with someone purely because of what they can offer you at a material, professional or social level.

Sun in Scorpio,
Venus in Capricorn

Emotionally reserved; still waters run deep; powerful
emotions kept under tight control.

Sun in Sagittarius,
Venus in Capricorn

An easy-going persona but emotionally cautious and
insecure; optimism battles with pessimism.

Sun in Capricorn,
Venus in Capricorn

Feelings are held in check; an emphasis on having
a good reputation and solid public image.

Sun in Aquarius,
Venus in Capricorn

You can be dispassionate and emotionally distant
when feeling insecure; an emphasis on logic.

Sun in Pisces,
Venus in Capricorn

Piscean over-sensitivity is tempered by Capricorn
common sense; loyal and steadfast.

Natal Venus
in Aquarius

For your chart or other people's, here is what it means to have Venus in Aquarius. This is the section where you'll find out how your Venus and Sun signs work together – and where they disagree.

Element	Mode	Keywords
Air	Fixed	Friendly, independent, altruistic

You like to take a slightly remote approach to everything connected with love, friendship and relationships. It's not that you're unemotional, exactly, but you need to keep a sense of distance between you and the rest of the world, and you quickly feel stifled if the atmosphere becomes too intense and highly charged. Any regular displays of jealousy, possessiveness or control from others will eventually make you want to run in the opposite direction as fast as possible. You can't bear the thought of being tied down or owned in any way, and you don't take kindly to being told what to do, either. If you're happy with someone, they will discover how loyal and trustworthy you can be. They might also learn how stubborn you are at times, determined to dig in your heels and not concede an iota, and then how you will suddenly completely change your mind about the whole thing. The prospect of change can alarm you, although sometimes you love the idea of throwing everything up in the air and seeing how it falls. There's no doubt that you can be a mass of contradictions, making it hard for anyone to take you for granted because they're never quite sure what they're dealing with on a day-to-day basis. The fact is that you love proving that you're an individual with your own set of idiosyncrasies.

You have a wonderful gift for friendship and enjoy getting to know people regardless of their social standing, politics or ethnic group. What matters to you is their particular take on life and their ability to hold an intelligent conversation. Anything else simply doesn't matter.

Sun in Sagittarius,
Venus in Aquarius

An emphasis on freedom, independence and
individualism; encouraging and supportive.

Sun in Capricorn,
Venus in Aquarius

A need for some form of emotional detachment;
cool, restrained and civilized.

Sun in Aquarius,
Venus in Aquarius

Very friendly and you seek out kindred spirits; often at
one step removed emotionally.

Sun in Pisces,
Venus in Aquarius

Considerate, kind and compassionate; charismatic;
idealistic but easily hurt and disappointed.

Sun in Aries,
Venus in Aquarius

High expectations of others; fun-loving and
independent; you love being an inspirational trailblazer.

Natal Venus in Pisces

What does it mean if you – or someone you know – were born with Venus in Pisces? You're about to find out. Planets don't work in isolation, so here you'll discover the sort of team that's made by your Venus and Sun signs.

Element	Mode	Keywords
Water	Mutable	Sensitive, escapist, romantic

You definitely wear rose-tinted glasses when it comes to love and romance. You long to be swept off your feet by your one true love, so you can both escape into your own little world and live happily ever after. Whenever real life starts to intrude on this Hollywood vision of romance, or you discover that your beloved has as many foibles as the rest of us, you can feel out of your depth and profoundly disappointed. You may even feel betrayed by the person who you originally thought was so perfect. It wasn't supposed to be like this! If things go really wrong and someone breaks your heart – and that can happen much more often than you care to admit – you must guard against a tendency to see yourself as a victim, martyr or someone who has sacrificed everything for love. Taking such an attitude will make it even more likely that you'll attract people who will exploit or upset you. It will be much more helpful if you can learn to set clear and strong emotional boundaries, so you no longer feel duty-bound to rescue every lame duck you encounter or get involved with someone simply because you feel sorry for them.

You have a tremendous appreciation of art and music, whether you're very creative yourself or you enjoy other people's work. Either way, it helps you to heal your sensitive emotions and recharge your emotional batteries, because if you don't do this you can become drained and flattened by life.

Sun in Capricorn,
Venus in Pisces

Your disciplined and serious image hides great
sensitivity; fear of being hurt or rejected.

Sun in Aquarius,
Venus in Pisces

Very kind and considerate; your rational Aquarian self
is often puzzled by your mysterious Piscean emotions.

Sun in Pisces,
Venus in Pisces

Ultra-sensitive and vulnerable; a need to strengthen
your emotional defences; otherworldly and escapist.

Sun in Aries,
Venus in Pisces

Idealistic and romantic, expecting the best from
everyone; can always be on the hunt for the next
big relationship.

Sun in Taurus,
Venus in Pisces

Piscean emotions are stabilized by Taurean steadiness;
kind, affectionate and faithful.

Venus in
the houses

In addition to your natal Venus falling into one of the twelve signs of the zodiac, it also sits in one of the twelve houses in your birth chart. Each house rules a different theme of life, such as home or friendships. The house position of your natal Venus describes the area of life with which your Venus has the greatest affinity. You must also consider the sign of your natal Venus, because this might be compatible with the house it occupies – but, then again, it might not.

If you have a rough idea of your time of birth, you can consult your chart (see page 174 on how to obtain your birth chart) to discover the house position of your Venus, and then look up its meaning here.

Venus in the 1st house: personal style

You place a lot of value on yourself: your pleasing appearance, the attractive image you create and the way you like to spend your time. Your natural charm and considerate attitude win you many friends, and you have an address book to prove it. Take care that you don't place so much importance on the way things (and people) look that you judge them accordingly. Excluding anything and anyone that isn't perfect means you will miss out in many ways.

Venus in the 2nd house: values

Money, wealth and possessions mean a great deal to you. Knowing that you have enough of all the material things in life gives you some much-needed emotional security. You enjoy spending money on beautiful objects, and the sign occupied by Venus will tell you whether you love to splurge or are careful with every penny. This is a wonderfully sensual and luxurious area for Venus, so you'll place a lot of importance on your sex life, too. Breaking up with someone is especially hard to do because you don't like change.

Venus in the 3rd house: communication style

You love a good chat! Of course, it helps that you're a born conversationalist and you have a great way with words. You're tactful and know how to say difficult things without causing offence. It's highly likely that you're a popular neighbour who enjoys keeping in touch with the people living nearby, as well as siblings and friends. Short journeys and shopping trips are good fun. You can't resist buying anything that helps you to keep in touch with the rest of the world, such as the latest phone or laptop, especially if it's just come on to the market. Books, magazines, podcasts, apps, downloads and clever gadgets all appeal, too.

Venus in the 4th house: home

Home is most definitely where your heart is and it's also your emotional refuge. If your family are there, too, or the people you regard as family in all but name, then so much the better. You have a deep yearning to be with the people you care about, and are in your element if you can cook for them or take care of them in some way. You could be a gifted interior decorator, too, with a knack for finding comfortable and beautiful furniture and fittings, especially if they have an old-world charm.

Venus in the 5th house: creativity

This is the most creative position for Venus. It shows that you're artistic and you enjoy expressing your many talents. What's more, this is the planet of love in the house of love, so you're naturally attuned to all things connected with matters of the heart. You need other people in your life, but they must be people that you really care about. They appreciate having you around, too, and it's highly likely that you're very popular and in great demand. Children are especially important to you.

Venus in the 6th house: work and health

Your working life is intrinsically bound up with your social life. Maybe you met your other half at work, or through a colleague, or perhaps some of your best friends have been your workmates. You might also meet friends or partners as the result of health-related matters. You have the happy gift of getting on well with people you work with, and you might also enjoy taking care of them or giving them a few words of advice every now and then. Watch your diet as too much rich food may not agree with you, leaving you feeling liverish.

Venus in the 7th house: relationships

Relationships mean everything to you. Without them, you'd wither like a flower without water. Luckily, you're unlikely to be left alone for long because you have many friends and admirers who are drawn to your charm and good manners. You prefer to have a long-term relationship rather than a series of flings. Having Venus in this house brings you popularity but it means you can struggle to stand up for yourself because you don't like upsetting anyone. Even if they've hurt your feelings, you don't like to hurt theirs.

Venus in the 8th house: intense emotions

There's an intensity to your emotions that may take people by surprise if other areas of your chart are more relaxed. In this house, Venus yearns for deep emotional meaning and a sense of profound connection with other people. This applies to friendships and family connections as well as sexual partnerships, which means that you don't take any relationship lightly. There may even be an element of possessiveness or jealousy in your relationships, and sex is likely to be an essential part of your life.

Venus in the 9th house: learning

You love life and have a great yearning for adventure. Travel, whether it's mental or physical, makes you happy. You adore visiting new places and discovering interesting ideas and philosophies. Friends and partners may come from a different background or culture to yours, or from another country. You have a lifelong love of learning, so adore burying yourself in books. It's quite likely that you have a strong belief system that acts as your guiding light and which you hope your partner will share.

Venus in the 10th house: reputation

Venus in this house suggests having friends in high places. They could be well-connected, influential or even famous, and you love it! You have a gift for getting to know the right people, making your address book the envy of everyone else. You may have a successful career in which you can express your artistic talents, or you might acquire a reputation for being a charming person to work with. You take love seriously and could be attracted to a partner who's a lot older or more influential than you.

Venus in the 11th house: networks

Friends are essential. You can't imagine being without them, and you've known many of them for almost your entire life. You're loyal and considerate towards them and you really value their company. Partners may have started off as friends, or you might meet your other half through one of your friends or through a favourite hobby. This emphasis on your friendships means that long-term partners must be equally keen on your friends and not be jealous if you choose to spend a lot of time with them.

Venus in the 12th house: retreat

You prefer to keep your emotions to yourself for much of the time, perhaps because they're private or you're worried about how they'll be received. This is a very sensitive position for Venus, making you emotionally vulnerable and easily hurt. You have deep reserves of compassion and empathy, and are especially tuned into anyone who's suffering, probably because you know only too well how that feels. You're a born romantic and an idealist, too, so are disappointed whenever the cold light of day intrudes on your dreams.

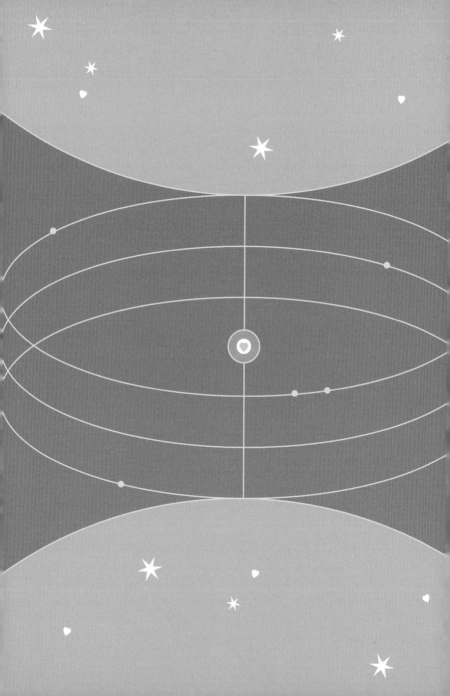

Part four

The Astrology of Mars

Here we're going to look at the role of Mars in your birth chart. This is the planet that governs our urges and desires, so it must be considered when examining the way you react to some of the people in your life. Mars represents what arouses us and puts the fire into our sex lives, so the sign occupied by Mars when you were born describes the way you go after what you want in love – and also in the rest of your life.

Mars can be hot stuff in more ways than one because this is also the planet that describes what triggers our fighting instinct and makes us seethe with rage. Read about your own Mars sign and how it combines with your Sun sign, as well as the position of Mars in the charts of some of the people in your life.

♂ What Mars represents in astrology

Action! Mars is not a planet that likes to sit around and twiddle its thumbs. It wants to be busy, to be occupied, to be motivated and driven. Mars is the hustler of the solar system, the planet that chivvies us along and stamps its foot when we aren't as quick on the draw as it expects. It is also the planet that rules sexual attraction and sexual gratification, so it's a very important player in relationships.

We all have Mars somewhere in our chart and the sign it occupies reveals a whole host of information about how we go after what we want in life. How about your Mars? Do you launch a full-blooded attack with little preparation, do you procrastinate and check the details before taking the first tentative steps, or do you ask someone else's opinion because you aren't sure of what you're doing? This applies to every area of life but in this book we're concerned about how Mars affects our ability to get on well with others.

Urges and desires

Even if this is your first foray into astrology, the astrological symbol for Mars might look familiar. That's because it's also the symbol for the male sex. This is a huge clue about Mars's action in relationships. It's the planet that governs our urges and desires, our passions, wants and needs, and how we satisfy them. When we aren't able to gratify them for some reason we often display another classic side of Mars – frustration and anger. These are also emotions that eventually crop up in almost every relationship, whether we like it or not. Mars, when sufficiently goaded, likes to stamp his feet or stage the kind of noisy argument that means the plaster is still falling from the ceiling hours later.

No wonder Mars is often regarded as the planetary equivalent of the rude and pushy guest at the astrological party. While his paramour Venus is checking her reflection to make sure she's looking good before striking up a conversation, Mars is squaring his shoulders, scanning the room, eyeing up the talent and then making a beeline for whoever grabs his attention.

The thrill of the chase

Mars adores being in pursuit of a quarry. This might be a hobby, career or new lover, but they can all have an impact on a partnership. For instance, if someone has Mars in a sign that's completely driven by ambition, this is bound to affect their relationships. Equally, a relationship will suffer if one partner is always searching for their next sexual conquest while neglecting their loved ones at home. Sometimes, the thrill of the chase is a lot more exciting than getting what we want, because then the fun is over. What can we do but embark on a new quest so we can recapture that buzz and surge of adrenalin. Is this you? It all depends on which sign your Mars occupies in your birth chart, so read on!

Natal Mars in Aries

How does natal Mars behave in Aries? Here's some vital information, whether you're the one with this placing or you're reading about someone you know. In this section you'll discover how this Mars connects with your Sun sign or that of someone in your life.

Element	Mode	Keywords
Fire	Cardinal	Fast, impatient, urgent

'I want it, and I want it now!' This is the essence of Mars in Aries. It doesn't want to hang about and wait. Who's got time for that? You have things to do, places to go and people to meet, and you don't want to be kept waiting. You want instant gratification, and the sooner the better. This can lead to hasty decisions and some rash judgements, and inevitably the odd mistake along the way. Do you learn from those mistakes? Not necessarily! You can be in too much of a hurry to move on to the next activity to pay much attention to what's just happened.

Mars is the planetary ruler of Aries, so this placing is a double dose of Martian energy. It doesn't take much to rouse your impatience and fiery temper, but your anger tends to flare up fast, blaze briefly and then die down again. Life is far too short to bear grudges. And anyway, you really enjoy the kissing and making-up stage of an argument.

When it comes to relationships, you're ardent and honest. You can't help showing your true feelings, so for others it's a case of what they see is what they get. You don't pretend, but that can sometimes cause problems if you fail to choose your words carefully enough. Aries is a sign that can be very self-centred, so that's something to guard against. It's one thing to have a strong sense of self and quite another to expect your own desires and requirements to always take precedence over everyone else's.

Sun in Aries, Mars in Aries

Active; impatient; prone to sudden tantrums; dynamic; daring; you take the initiative; passionate; sexy.

Sun in Taurus, Mars in Aries

A mix of Taurean steadiness and Aries haste; you need a sense of purpose; loyal and loving.

Sun in Gemini, Mars in Aries

Lively; gregarious; inquisitive; positive; you desire a stimulating relationship; easily bored.

Sun in Cancer, Mars in Aries

Motivated; affectionate; protective of loved ones; feelings are easily hurt.

Sun in Leo, Mars in Aries

Demonstrative; sociable; fun-loving; competitive; full of passion and drama; loving and romantic.

Sun in Virgo, Mars in Aries

Virgo caution clashes with Aries urgency; you can be sexually unrestrained in the right circumstances.

Sun in Libra, Mars in Aries

Strong need for partnerships versus desire for independence; romantic; idealistic.

Sun in Scorpio, Mars in Aries

Powerful and intense emotions that can be hidden; sex and anger can go together.

Sun in Sagittarius, Mars in Aries

Carefree, freedom-loving; you hate being emotionally restricted; adventurous.

Sun in Capricorn, Mars in Aries

Hard-working, competitive; a desire to get ahead, possibly at the expense of relationships.

Sun in Aquarius, Mars in Aries

Original, quirky; idealistic; you want to be in charge emotionally; determined.

Sun in Pisces, Mars in Aries

Sensitive, kind; you desire sexual and emotional variety; partner must be inventive.

Natal Mars in Taurus

When your natal Mars is in Taurus, what does that mean about how Mars connects with your Sun sign or that of someone in your life? Find out here.

Element	Mode	Keywords
Earth	Fixed	Steady, practical, possessive

We have a strange combination here, because Mars is all about action and Taurus is all about taking its time. So how does that work? It can mean that you deliberate about what to do and how to go about it, and you refuse to be rushed. You'll get there in your own sweet time, thank you very much, and anyone who's foolish enough to chivvy you along will soon experience the stubborn attitude that is so characteristic of Taurus. You have a pronounced ability to plant both feet firmly on the ground and refuse to budge. And the more someone tries to make you change your mind, the more you'll resist until you finally lose your temper.

One of your greatest gifts is your practical approach to life. You're an ideal person to know in a crisis because you're calm, pragmatic and reliable. Yes, you may be quaking on the inside but that's not the impression you give to others unless they can read the signs.

It's important for you to make your own way in the world, rather than rely on other people for hand-outs, so you're a willing and industrious worker. Taurus has a strong connection with finance and you may enjoy earning money because of what it can buy you and your loved ones. You may even want to be the main or sole breadwinner, because you feel you should be the one who provides for your family. This can sometimes lead to a possessive attitude towards loved ones, and at its worst it can almost be as though you've bought and paid for them so now they belong to you. Unsurprisingly, this can be a source of friction!

Sun in Aries, Mars in Taurus

Aries impatience tempered by Taurean control; strong sex drive; loving and affectionate.

Sun in Taurus, Mars in Taurus

Sensual, passionate, sexy; can be stubborn and intransigent; must guard against possessiveness.

Sun in Gemini, Mars in Taurus

Gemini restlessness clashes with Taurean stability; at best, great for grounding Gemini flightiness.

Sun in Cancer, Mars in Taurus

Strong desire for emotional and material security; home is where the heart is.

Sun in Leo, Mars in Taurus

Proud, loyal but obstinate; determined; family-minded and traditional; sexy and romantic.

Sun in Virgo, Mars in Taurus

Grounded, practical, methodical; Virgoan industry can be slowed down by Taurean lethargy; loving and kind.

Sun in Libra, Mars in Taurus

Earthy Taurus tempered by Libran refinement; highly sensual in the right circumstances.

Sun in Scorpio, Mars in Taurus

Powerful emotional drive; hidden reactions which are gradually expressed; potential for jealousy and possessiveness.

Sun in Sagittarius, Mars in Taurus

You want space and room to breathe, yet also need to stick to the status quo; inspired by causes and enthusiasms.

Sun in Capricorn, Mars in Taurus

Desire to create the right impression by following convention; very hard-working; materialistic.

Sun in Aquarius, Mars in Taurus

Awkward blend of Aquarian independence and Taurean dependence; capable of immense obstinacy.

Sun in Pisces, Mars in Taurus

Romantic and affectionate; Taurean practicality can ground or stifle Piscean wistfulness and escapism.

Natal Mars in Gemini

If your natal Mars falls in Gemini, how does it behave? How does that affect your relationships? Or perhaps you are trying to work out what makes a friend or loved one tick. Here's some vital information on how this Mars connects with your Sun sign or that of someone in your life.

Element	Mode	Keywords
Air	Mutable	Variety, clever communication, versatility

You certainly have a way with words. You use them to get ahead in the world, whether through your work or simply as a result of clever debate and running verbal rings around friends and family. Mars is a competitive planet and you like to compete with other people through conversation, especially when it comes to showing off your brain power and winning arguments. Try not to revert to too much sarcasm, though. This verbal competition may have started at an early age, with family conversations that sharpened your mental abilities and taught you how to argue your corner, especially with brothers and sisters. Sibling rivalry could have been invented by you!

That Gemini restlessness gives you the urge to keep on the move as much as possible. Life must offer you plenty of variety and change, otherwise you're quickly bored. Cars, motorbikes, bicycles and brisk walks all appeal because you need to be able to get around independently whenever possible and often on a sudden whim. You enjoy having some company on these trips but hate having to hang around waiting for other people to get ready. It's such a waste of time! Although you enjoy having some time alone you must balance that by getting together with people on your wavelength. If you live alone, you enjoy making contact with the rest of the world through your phone or computer, and may get involved in spirited or even bad-tempered discussions on social media.

Sun in Aries, Mars in Gemini

Lively, inquisitive; self-motivated but can lose interest; you love speed, such as fast cars or motorbikes.

Sun in Taurus, Mars in Gemini

Stable Taurus enlivened by quick-thinking Gemini; caught between the safety of the old and attraction of the new.

Sun in Gemini, Mars in Gemini

Sparky; versatile; intelligent; clever conversationalist; easily bored and needs mental stimulation.

Sun in Cancer, Mars in Gemini

Home life is important but not always peaceful; you want a stable domestic base but with some independence.

Sun in Leo, Mars in Gemini

Entertaining companion, sociable; full of enthusiasms that may be fleeting; you love to shine in a group.

Sun in Virgo, Mars in Gemini

Intelligent; attention to detail can lead to anxiety; strong nervous energy that needs positive outlets.

Sun in Libra, Mars in Gemini

Charming, articulate; Libran tact counters Gemini sarcasm; partner must have brains and wit.

Sun in Scorpio, Mars in Gemini

Deep Scorpio emotions may be glossed over or joked about; a formidable opponent in arguments.

Sun in Sagittarius, Mars in Gemini

You love travel and being a free agent; enjoys sharing ideas and viewpoints; flirty and entertaining.

Sun in Capricorn, Mars in Gemini

Bright, intelligent; very dry sense of humour; Capricorn seriousness lightened by Gemini sparkle.

Sun in Aquarius, Mars in Gemini

Clever; you don't suffer fools gladly; friends and partners must be intellectual equals; can be opinionated.

Sun in Pisces, Mars in Gemini

Changeable; interested in many things but may not delve deeply into any of them; loving but not always faithful.

Natal Mars in Cancer

This section will tell you all about how natal Mars behaves in Cancer – vital information that will help in your relationships, whether you're the one with this placing or you're reading about someone you know.

Element	Mode	Keywords
Water	Cardinal	Defensive, faithful, tenacious

The key to understanding your Mars sign is to compare it to a crab. There it is, cosily nestled under its favourite rock in the sea, preferably with the rest of its family. It scuttles out to collect food and then dashes back in again. After all, that shell protects some very succulent flesh from predators so the crab must feel safe. When alarmed or threatened, it waves its pincers in a menacing fashion until either the problem goes away or there's an all-out battle. This is classic Mars in Cancer behaviour – you like to feel comfortable and protected, and you need a safe retreat from the rest of the world. When under threat, you can be defensive or moody, or you rise to the challenge and give as good as you get.

You may even display a rather crusty or stiff persona at times, just like the crab's shell, but it's purely for protective reasons. It's because you're scared of getting hurt or being let down, so sometimes you overcompensate by appearing offhand or withdrawn. However, once someone has gained your trust, they discover how delightfully warm, loving, considerate and kind you really are. The fact is that other people are essential to your happiness, especially if they're your nearest and dearest. Enjoying a happy family life is vitally important to you, whether it consists of blood relatives or friends who you've adopted as your family in all but name. You will go through thick and thin for them, but you expect the same commitment in return and feel deeply betrayed if you don't get it.

Sun in Aries, Mars in Cancer

Motivated, determined;
can be moody and irritable; warm,
expansive and affectionate.

Sun in Taurus, Mars in Cancer

You want a settled and happy home
life; loving and dependable; can be
possessive and clingy.

Sun in Gemini, Mars in Cancer

Bright and witty, with underlying
kindness and compassion; partner
must also be a good friend.

Sun in Cancer, Mars in Cancer

Strong desire for a stable
domestic life; tenacious in
relationships and can be
subtly needy.

Sun in Leo, Mars in Cancer

Protective of loved ones and
will fight their corner; loving
and openly affectionate; can be
emotionally demanding.

Sun in Virgo, Mars in Cancer

Practical and organized, especially
domestically; initial reserve and
caution give way to warmth
and protectiveness.

Sun in Libra, Mars in Cancer

Courteous and considerate; Libran
distaste for emotional displays clashes
with Cancerian desire to show deep love.

Sun in Scorpio, Mars in Cancer

Powerful and profound emotions that
are often hidden; highly emotional
and can be moody.

Sun in Sagittarius, Mars in Cancer

At best, an ability to express Sagittarian
wanderlust while honouring the
Cancerian need for a secure home base.

Sun in Capricorn, Mars in Cancer

You work hard to create and
maintain a stable home; ambitions
can clash with domesticity; fear of
emotional rejection.

Sun in Aquarius, Mars in Cancer

Detached and rational
persona hides deep emotional
reserves; urge to mother friends
as well as family.

Sun in Pisces, Mars in Cancer

Very sensitive and intuitive;
empathetic and compassionate; can
be swept up in big emotional dramas.

Natal Mars in Leo

How does natal Mars behave when it's in the sign of Leo? Here is some crucial information, whether you're the one with this placing or you're reading about someone you know. Find out here how this Mars connects with your Sun sign or that of someone in your life.

Element	Mode	Keywords
Fire	Fixed	Powerful, pleasure-loving, sociable

This is a very stately and majestic placing for Mars, especially if you have other planets in Leo. You have innate pride and a strong sense of your own self-worth which is reflected in almost everything you do. Creative activities are especially valuable because they give you the scope to express yourself imaginatively, particularly if you feel that some of your emotions aren't very nice or show you in a poor light. Maybe you could channel them into an artistic creation instead?

Having people around you is essential to your happiness, provided, of course, that you care about them. If you don't, you really can't be bothered. You need a solid family unit or a group of good friends you can rely on and who won't let you down. They can also bolster your ego whenever it's taken a knock because even though you give the impression of being self-sufficient you're much more sensitive than you like to admit, so put-downs and unkind words go deep. They may even continue to rankle long after everyone else has forgotten what the fuss was about.

Any planet in Leo likes to be noticed so some element of self-centredness is inevitable, but you must guard against any tendency to become so involved in your own life that you come across as self-obsessed. The spotlight can't always be on you! You flourish whenever someone showers you with love and adoration, but it must be genuinely reciprocated otherwise the relationship will struggle to survive.

Sun in Aries, Mars in Leo

Enthusiastic, warm-hearted; must be able to do your own thing and not be held back; innovative; quick-tempered.

Sun in Taurus, Mars in Leo

You desire a stable and comfortable life; resistant to change and surprises; loving but can be controlling.

Sun in Gemini, Mars in Leo

Lively, sociable; charismatic; good at combining ideas with action; Gemini coolness warmed by Leo fire.

Sun in Cancer, Mars in Leo

Family-minded and you want a solid domestic base; protective of loved ones but mustn't be too demanding.

Sun in Leo, Mars in Leo

Creativity needs positive outlets; a desire for applause and attention; strong sense of pride; very affectionate.

Sun in Virgo, Mars in Leo

Virgo reticence vies with Leo self-confidence; warm emotions; excellent organizational skills.

Sun in Libra, Mars in Leo

Libran charm mixed with Leo warmth; you adore making and receiving romantic gestures.

Sun in Scorpio, Mars in Leo

Strong-willed and determined; you hate being contradicted; emotions go deep and are carefully controlled.

Sun in Sagittarius, Mars in Leo

Warm, fun-loving, easy-going; you enjoy travel and socializing; loving and kind.

Sun in Capricorn, Mars in Leo

A strong drive for success and achievement can dominate relationships; you enjoy a grand passion.

Sun in Aquarius, Mars in Leo

Aquarian aloofness warmed by Leo affection; friendships can turn into romance or sex.

Sun in Pisces, Mars in Leo

You try to control excessive emotions; kind and considerate; full of empathy; romantic and idealistic.

Natal Mars in Virgo

When your natal Mars is in Virgo, how does it behave? Here's some vital information, whether you're the one with this placing or you're reading about someone you know. This is where you will find out how the connection influences anyone coming under this combination of sign and planet.

Element	Mode	Keywords
Earth	Mutable	Fastidious, practical, helpful

Virgo is renowned for its perfectionism and you have a strong urge to make many areas of your life as flawless as possible. That includes your relationships, whether they're with family, children, colleagues, friends, lovers or a long-term partner. Anything slipshod or half-hearted feels as uncomfortable as a stone in your shoe, so you have very high standards of behaviour and are furious with yourself whenever you feel you've let those standards slide. You are equally annoyed if you suspect that someone in your life isn't doing their bit, and will quickly point out where you think they've gone wrong. This is giving valuable advice, as far as you're concerned, but it can feel like irritable or even scathing nagging to anyone on the receiving end of it.

Your practical skills are second to none, so you're the person to turn to in a crisis or when someone needs a helping hand. However, your sense of duty and obligation can mean that you don't know where to draw the line and can end up making yourself ill through overwork or devoting too much time to others and not enough to yourself. Do you remember the advice given in planes that if there's a problem with the air supply you should put on your own oxygen mask before helping others to put on theirs? The same is true in the rest of your life, because you can't be of service in the way you'd like if you're feeling exhausted or drained. Strangely enough, doing too little can be as bad for you as doing too much, because being inactive or sedentary can lead to an excess of nervous energy that leaves you unable to relax. So you should strive for moderation in all things. Easier said than done?

Sun in Aries, Mars in Virgo

Aries haste clashes with Virgo caution; has stamina and staying power when getting things done.

Sun in Taurus, Mars in Virgo

Reliable, practical; earthy, grounded and stable; you need solid relationships with people who can be trusted.

Sun in Gemini, Mars in Virgo

Intelligent; an inquiring mind; restless and nervy; you enjoy conversations but can struggle to discuss emotional matters.

Sun in Cancer, Mars in Virgo

Caring, helpful and supportive; emphasis on creating the perfect home; highly strung.

Sun in Leo, Mars in Virgo

Great organizational skills; you need to be appreciated but Leo ego is controlled by Virgo modesty.

Sun in Virgo, Mars in Virgo

Assiduous, hard-working; difficult to relax and stop being on duty; can be acutely critical towards loved ones.

Sun in Libra, Mars in Virgo

High standards of behaviour and courtesy; your own worst critic; embarrassed by big emotional displays.

Sun in Scorpio, Mars in Virgo

Highly driven and motivated; must be able to express complex Scorpio emotions and not stifle them.

Sun in Sagittarius, Mars in Virgo

You need the freedom to be yourself, even if that isn't perfect; need an intelligent and witty partner.

Sun in Capricorn, Mars in Virgo

Self-sufficient and reliable; may only express your emotions when you feel safe and won't be ridiculed.

Sun in Aquarius, Mars in Virgo

Clever; you know your own mind and aren't afraid to share it with others; emotionally reserved.

Sun in Pisces, Mars in Virgo

Piscean emotional excesses held in check by Virgoan sense of propriety; must learn to trust yourself and others.

Natal Mars in Libra

Here's some vital information on how Mars in Libra affects your personality and attitude to relationships. In this section you will discover how this Mars connects with your Sun sign or that of someone in your life.

Element	Mode	Keywords
Air	Cardinal	Diplomatic, considerate, focused on relationships

Assertive and sometimes downright argumentative, Mars is uneasy in the courteous sign of Libra, with its emphasis on good manners, harmony and creating a favourable impression. This fiery planet struggles to express itself fully when it's always expected to be on its best behaviour, resulting in you feeling infuriated and frustrated. Libra is the sign that likes to concentrate on other people rather than itself, so it may go completely against the grain to make a direct request for what you want. One invaluable way around this is through the gentle art of Libran persuasion. You instinctively know how to appeal to others and win them over, whether that's through flattery, charm or some other diplomatic strategy. Half the time, you may not even be aware of what you're doing because it comes so easily to you.

Relationships are a major focus for you. You want them to be enjoyable, successful and civilized, and you work hard to make them so. If a partner or friend fails to reciprocate, or isn't as polite or considerate as you usually try to be, you can feel very annoyed because it doesn't strike you as fair. You've put in all that effort so why can't they do the same? Any sort of injustice gets to you, whether it's personal or something you read about in a newspaper, and even if you find it difficult to stand up for yourself because you don't want to cause offence you have no qualms about defending other people if they're being mistreated. You may even make a very successful career out of it.

Sun in Aries, Mars in Libra

Conflict between wanting to please yourself and please others; arguments with a partner can be a form of foreplay.

Sun in Taurus, Mars in Libra

You like to take life gently whenever possible; resistant to change; emphasis on looking good and being liked.

Sun in Gemini, Mars in Libra

Sociable; a clever way with words; partners must be intelligent and not too emotionally demanding.

Sun in Cancer, Mars in Libra

Focused and ambitious; can be defensive and huffy when feelings are hurt; fiercely protective of others.

Sun in Leo, Mars in Libra

You love to be with others; you want easy-going relationships that will last; can be overly romantic and idealistic.

Sun in Virgo, Mars in Libra

Virgo high standards can upset others; partner must be cultured, polite and well-mannered.

Sun in Libra, Mars in Libra

Strong focus on pleasing others can eventually lead to resentment if your needs are not met in return; great desire for partnership.

Sun in Scorpio, Mars in Libra

Scorpio intensity regulated by Libran distaste for big emotional showdowns; can be very persuasive.

Sun in Sagittarius, Mars in Libra

Friendly and generous; fall in love easily but partner must be intelligent; you enjoy having a cause to fight for.

Sun in Capricorn, Mars in Libra

Ambitious, motivated; you get ahead by knowing the 'right' people; emphasis on impressing others.

Sun in Aquarius, Mars in Libra

Drawn to people who are clever and attractive; uncomfortable with excessively emotional displays.

Sun in Pisces, Mars in Libra

Easily bowled over emotionally; idealistic and expects the best from partners; considerate.

Natal Mars in Scorpio

On these pages you'll find out how Mars in Scorpio connects with your Sun sign or that of someone in your life. How does natal Mars behave in Scorpio? Here's some vital information, whether you're the one with this placing or you're reading about someone you know.

Element	Mode	Keywords
Water	Fixed	Impassioned, profound, strong-willed

Life takes on an all-or-nothing quality when you have Mars in Scorpio. Mars is the co-ruler of Scorpio and was its sole ruler until the discovery of Pluto, so it is very much at home in this sign. As a result, your Mars in Scorpio characteristics are so strong that they filter into just about every area of your life. You channel a huge amount of energy into everything you do, whether it's hunting out a bargain online or planning your next coup at work, and you expect everyone else to be equally committed. You're very disappointed – or angry – if they aren't, and you can't fathom their attitude. Your tendency to see the world in very black and white terms makes it difficult for you to compromise if you don't agree with someone. You can't understand why they don't see things your way, and you'll eventually become furious if you continue to fail to see eye to eye with each other.

Every Mars placing has potential, but this one has a lot more than most. There's almost nothing you can't do if you put your mind to it. However, as is so often the case with Scorpio, this potential must be given full scope and expression, and allowed to develop in whichever way is most positive, otherwise you end up feeling thwarted and frustrated. This can lead to obsession, resentment and ultimately a desire for revenge.

The intensity and deep emotions of Scorpio are always simmering away inside you, even if you take care to keep them hidden as much as possible. After all, you like to play your cards close to your chest and only reveal your feelings on a need-to-know basis. It feels safer that way.

Sun in Aries, Mars in Scorpio

A powerhouse of energy, not always controlled; drive and motivation must be channelled in the right directions.

Sun in Taurus, Mars in Scorpio

Taurean placidity clashes with Scorpio intensity; loving and very loyal; must control possessive tendencies.

Sun in Gemini, Mars in Scorpio

Gemini versatility plus Scorpio staying power; in relationships can veer between fidelity and fickleness.

Sun in Cancer, Mars in Scorpio

Powerful emotions that are carefully protected; you take time to trust someone but are then devoted to them.

Sun in Leo, Mars in Scorpio

You take relationships very seriously; extremely loyal and committed; can be stubborn and inflexible.

Sun in Virgo, Mars in Scorpio

Can be emotionally remote; high level of nervous energy can lead to worry and obsessiveness.

Sun in Libra, Mars in Scorpio

Deepest and messiest emotions are kept under tight control; Libra can be uncomfortable with Scorpio intensity.

Sun in Scorpio, Mars in Scorpio

Profound feelings that may never be fully explored or expressed; you keep tight hold of personal secrets.

Sun in Sagittarius, Mars in Scorpio

Capable of great depths of emotion and wisdom that comes from experience; dedicated to causes.

Sun in Capricorn, Mars in Scorpio

Reserved and controlled; you take life seriously; great sense of humour; dependable and stoic.

Sun in Aquarius, Mars in Scorpio

Aquarian emotional detachment clashes with Scorpio complexity; loyal and affectionate; stubborn and opinionated.

Sun in Pisces, Mars in Scorpio

Feelings go deep but can be too complex or mysterious to fully express; can be very secretive; you guard your privacy.

Natal Mars in Sagittarius

When natal Mars is in Sagittarius, it will connect with your Sun sign – or that of a friend or partner – in a specific way. This section helps you understand and make the best use of that knowledge.

Element	Mode	Keywords
Fire	Mutable	Adventurous, blunt, enthusiastic

Honesty is one of your biggest strengths, because you can't bear the thought of fudging the truth or, even worse, telling lies. You like to say it how it is, even if other people don't like what they hear. However, your desire to be honest and straightforward can sometimes cause ructions because of your inability to mince your words or tone down your opinions. When you're roused by Sagittarian enthusiasm and confidence to the point of not realizing what you're saying, you can be blunt, tactless or arrogant. Or all three! You can also be withering if you disagree with someone's opinions, pointing out all the holes in their arguments and taking the moral high ground if you think it's necessary – which it often seems to be.

On a positive note – and that's never far away because Sagittarius is a very positive sign – you're powered by optimism and enthusiasm. Your glass is always half-full – unless other areas of your chart tell a very different story – and you grab hold of adventure at every opportunity. You might also be an intrepid traveller, always choosing to visit another exotic part of the globe where you soak up the local atmosphere rather than returning to the same place year after year. That would be so boring! Mental journeys, whether through further education, philosophy or politics, can also appeal to you, in which case you might even get quite competitive about how much you know about a particular subject. If you're to satisfy your Mars sign, you must always find fresh challenges to aim at. You may not always hit the target but at least you have great fun in the process.

Sun in Aries,
Mars in Sagittarius

Enthusiastic, ebullient, energetic; can be too gung-ho about potential risks; must have a lively partner.

Sun in Taurus,
Mars in Sagittarius

Torn between playing safe and taking risks; Taurean possessiveness relieved by Sagittarian desire for freedom.

Sun in Gemini,
Mars in Sagittarius

Lively; intelligent; independent; friendly and loving but hates feeling tied down; intrigued by ideas and knowledge.

Sun in Cancer,
Mars in Sagittarius

Cancerian longing for home and emotional security clashes with Sagittarian desire for the wide open spaces.

Sun in Leo,
Mars in Sagittarius

Loving, warm-hearted and affectionate; supportive; proud; expansive; enthusiastic.

Sun in Virgo,
Mars in Sagittarius

Virgoan eye for detail versus Sagittarian desire to see the big picture; desire for change and variety; articulate.

Sun in Libra,
Mars in Sagittarius

Libran diplomacy helps to counter Sagittarian gaffes; friends and partners must be able to think for themselves.

Sun in Scorpio,
Mars in Sagittarius

Scorpio privacy versus Sagittarian openness; reduction in Scorpio possessiveness; you need something to believe in.

Sun in Sagittarius,
Mars in Sagittarius

Enthusiastic and expansive; optimistic; friendly and loving; can fight for beliefs or causes; independent.

Sun in Capricorn,
Mars in Sagittarius

Capricorn seriousness lightened by Sagittarian sense of fun; supportive and can be very wise.

Sun in Aquarius,
Mars in Sagittarius

You enjoy friendships and being with kindred spirits; interested in ideas and finding own path through life.

Sun in Pisces,
Mars in Sagittarius

Changeable; enthusiastic; impressionable; you want stimulating company and kindred spirits; may not always be faithful.

Natal Mars in Capricorn

How does natal Mars behave when it falls in Capricorn? Here's some vital information, whether you're the one with this combination or you're reading about someone you know. Here you'll discover how this Mars connects with your Sun sign or that of someone in your life.

Element	Mode	Keywords
Earth	Cardinal	Determined, ambitious, controlled

Life can be a serious business for you. And sometimes it's literally a business, thanks to your ambition and drive. For some with Mars in Capricorn, work is the be-all and end-all. This could be because they enjoy it so much that it's part of everything they do, or because of the status it promises to bring, or maybe a bit of both. Regardless of where you fit on this work ethic ladder, you have tremendous determination, drive and motivation. They spur you on through thick and thin – and sometimes life can seem remarkably thin, especially leading up to your late twenties – until you finally get where you want to go. Some signs might give up long before this through sheer frustration, but Capricorn is well equipped to slog away until it finally achieves its ambitions. This wins you great respect in the eyes of other people, and that's another bonus as far as you're concerned.

All of this takes a lot of self-control and discipline, which happily are two qualities that you have in abundance. You may even scale down other areas of your life in order to concentrate on whatever you consider to be most important emotionally or socially, or so you can focus on getting ahead materially. The Beatles may have reminded us that money can't buy us love, but it can certainly help you to acquire a lot of other things that make you feel good. However much you may enjoy your new car or giant TV set, you can't cuddle up with it in bed at night, so ideally you need a loving and supportive partner who can remind you that success doesn't only revolve around your job or bank balance but also involves a happy and fulfilling personal life.

Sun in Aries, Mars in Capricorn

Highly motivated, with Aries enterprise steadied by Capricorn doggedness; highly sexed with the right person.

Sun in Taurus, Mars in Capricorn

You have the ambition and drive to succeed; loyal and supportive; must guard against being too materialistic.

Sun in Gemini, Mars in Capricorn

Great communication skills backed up by iron determination; emotions can be held in check.

Sun in Cancer, Mars in Capricorn

Traditional values, both materially and emotionally; you want a stable domestic life and a successful career.

Sun in Leo, Mars in Capricorn

Organized and authoritative but can be bossy and inflexible; highly ambitious; will work hard to support loved ones.

Sun in Virgo, Mars in Capricorn

Dependable and reliable, but can work too hard; practical; shows love through actions rather than words.

Sun in Libra, Mars in Capricorn

Emphasis on doing things the right way so as to win respect; diplomatic and kind but can also be calculating.

Sun in Scorpio, Mars in Capricorn

Tremendous urge to get ahead, even if relationships suffer; can be emotionally guarded; very erotic in private.

Sun in Sagittarius, Mars in Capricorn

Sagittarian curiosity boosted by Capricorn impetus and purpose; torn between being a free spirit and following the rules.

Sun in Capricorn, Mars in Capricorn

Highly motivated; emphasis on reputation and respect; emotional life can play second fiddle to big ambitions.

Sun in Aquarius, Mars in Capricorn

Focus on rationality, common sense and seeing is believing; can be emotionally remote or withdrawn.

Sun in Pisces, Mars in Capricorn

At best, grounded and creative but can also be limited by fears; marvellous at putting compassion into action.

Natal Mars in Aquarius

How does the combination of natal Mars work out in the sign of Aquarius? Here's some vital information, whether you're the one with this placing or you're reading about someone you know. Here you'll discover how this Mars connects with your Sun sign or that of someone in your life.

Element	Mode	Keywords
Air	Fixed	Radical, detached, independent

The combination of dynamic Mars and independent Aquarius gives you an overwhelming urge to do your own thing in your own way. It's a tooth-grinding experience if someone tells you what to do or how to behave, even if circumstances mean that you have to toe the line – or appear to do so, while quietly continuing with your own agenda. Ideally, you want the opportunity to live your life in the way you choose, regardless of what others think or say. This isn't always a recipe for domestic harmony, unfortunately, so there could be plenty of arguments or battles of will whenever you fail to see eye to eye. You may even decide that it's better to live alone, especially if your Venus is in a sign that's equally emotionally detached, because then you don't have to cope with other people's high expectations and the resulting criticisms and scenes when those hopes are dashed. This doesn't mean you've abandoned the idea of falling in love, simply that you want to keep a little distance between you and your beloved. It could add a lot of sizzle and spice to your relationship – not to mention save you having to replace the china every time you throw it at each other.

You have a very independent streak but you're also unpredictable, which leaves others never quite sure about how or why you want to assert your freedom. One thing they can count on is your determination to champion and fight for a better world, especially if that involves protecting animals or defending human rights. Another given is the importance you place on your friendships and your need to mix with kindred spirits who share your hopes and dreams.

Sun in Aries,
Mars in Aquarius

Individualistic, with a love of freedom;
you embrace new enthusiasms but
may not follow them through.

Sun in Taurus,
Mars in Aquarius

Clash between Taurean love of
tradition and Aquarian iconoclasm;
loyal but can be obstinate.

Sun in Gemini,
Mars in Aquarius

Tremendous need for intellectual
freedom; drawn to quick and clever
people who can think for themselves.

Sun in Cancer,
Mars in Aquarius

Love of home clashes with the urge
to be a free spirit; must reconcile
need to show emotions with desire to
remain detached.

Sun in Leo,
Mars in Aquarius

Extremely loyal and steadfast
towards loved ones; strong sense of
pride can lead to determination to
have your own way.

Sun in Virgo,
Mars in Aquarius

You like to retain an air of aloofness
and detachment; may prefer to live
alone; strong opinions.

Sun in Libra,
Mars in Aquarius

Prefers the company of civilized and
intelligent people; strong desire to play
fair and treat everyone as your equal.

Sun in Scorpio,
Mars in Aquarius

Scorpio nature can be held in check
and controlled to avoid unpleasant
scenes, which can trigger frustration.

Sun in Sagittarius,
Mars in Aquarius

Strong drive to be independent;
excited by ideas and challenges;
partner must give you breathing space.

Sun in Capricorn,
Mars in Aquarius

Can be torn between convention
and rebellion; must find your own
way through life and on your
own terms.

Sun in Aquarius,
Mars in Aquarius

Can have a radical approach
to life; fiercely self-sufficient with
a dread of being tied down
or constrained.

Sun in Pisces,
Mars in Aquarius

Deeply humanitarian and altruistic;
may be happiest when fighting for a
cause you truly believe in.

Natal Mars in Pisces

How does natal Mars behave in Pisces? Here's some vital information, whether you're the one with this combination in your birth chart or you're looking up data on someone else. How Mars connects with your Sun sign is outlined on these pages.

Element	Mode	Keywords
Water	Mutable	Idealistic, altruistic, emotional

Let's get the not-so-good news out of the way first. Aggressive Mars is easily confused in dreamy Pisces, especially when its get up and go vanishes in the swirling mists of all that emotion and escapism. As a result, you may sometimes struggle to get yourself motivated, or could find that you begin an enterprise with great energy but all your enthusiasm gets snuffed out for reasons that you can't explain. At worst, this can leave you feeling adrift and rudderless, or you become heavily influenced by people who start telling you what to do, even if it isn't good for you.

It's essential that you find your own ways to get the best out of this very sensitive Mars placing. One option is to take care of others, whether they're humans, animals or plants. This noble instinct is a great expression of your very caring nature, but you must make sure you don't let this innate kindness turn into an obsessive urge to rescue every lost soul and lame duck that crosses your path. It's an impossible task and you risk becoming completely drained in the process. Pisces is the sign of self-sacrifice but that doesn't mean you should let every underdog bleed you dry until you have nothing left to offer. Ultimately, you must learn to take care of yourself and to know your limits, and then strengthen your boundaries so you're able to say 'no' and mean it.

You have tremendous creative and artistic potential, so give it full rein. Dance, music and art could appeal to you, or you might prefer to explore more esoteric topics such as meditation, religion or dream work, provided that you stay grounded while doing so.

Sun in Aries, Mars in Pisces

Aries bravado hides Piscean sensitivity; idealistic and romantic; must draw on Aries motivation and energy.

Sun in Libra, Mars in Pisces

Desire for romance and perfect love that can become a life-long quest; courteous; easily influenced by others.

Sun in Taurus, Mars in Pisces

Taurean stability helps to give direction to dreamy Pisces; artistic; can be very seductive and sensual.

Sun in Scorpio, Mars in Pisces

Emotional depths that may never be fully explored for fear of what you might find; immense intuition and sensitivity.

Sun in Gemini, Mars in Pisces

You need to express versatility and changeability; you want structure but not an energy-sapping routine.

Sun in Sagittarius, Mars in Pisces

Playful and lively; a positive approach to life but can be easily deterred by setbacks.

Sun in Cancer, Mars in Pisces

Sensitive and emotional; moody; you absorb the surrounding atmosphere like psychic blotting paper.

Sun in Capricorn, Mars in Pisces

Capricorn ambition gives focus to Piscean idealism; supportive of loved ones; prone to feeling shy.

Sun in Leo, Mars in Pisces

Kind, considerate and affectionate; creative gifts; high expectations of loved ones.

Sun in Aquarius, Mars in Pisces

High personal ideals and standards; altruistic and kind; can be emotionally absent or detached.

Sun in Virgo, Mars in Pisces

At best, Virgo practicality provides structure for escapist Pisces; at worst, can be endlessly disappointed in yourself.

Sun in Pisces, Mars in Pisces

Inspired and idealistic but can struggle to find motivation; easily influenced by others for good or ill; romantic.

Mars in the houses

The house that Mars occupies in your birth chart describes the area of life into which you instinctively channel your energies. This may also be the part of life that you feel most strongly about, or which is the greatest source of tension or disagreement for you.

Mars in the 1st house: personal style

You're always in a hurry. You hate having to wait for anything, especially if you know full well who's holding you up. This will quickly lead to impatience and temper tantrums, which can disrupt or mar relationships. You're often hasty, rushing into decisions without thinking them through properly. Who's got time for planning? Not you! You excel at leadership, being a pioneer and taking risks, but you also have an accident-prone streak and you don't always learn from your mistakes.

Mars in the 2nd house: values

You like to channel your considerable energies into whatever you consider to be important. This could be something materialistic, such as earning or saving money or owning your own home, or it might be more philosophical or spiritual, depending on Mars's sign. Whatever it is, you expect quick results and can have a very impulsive streak when it comes to spending money. In relationships, you must guard against irritable displays of possessiveness and placing too much emphasis on acquisitions.

Mars in the 3rd house: communication style

An abundance of nervous energy keeps you on your toes. You love being on the move, especially if that means driving a fast car or going for a jog. It's essential that you find positive outlets for all this energy and impetus, otherwise you can get drawn into bickering sessions or heated arguments which you're always absolutely determined to win. Watch out that your sharp tongue and cutting remarks don't cause unnecessary hurt or drive a permanent wedge between you and others.

Mars in the 4th house: home

Your home and family take up a lot of energy. That could be because you love being busy with DIY, gardening or really enthusiastic housework – these sorts of activities help you to ground your emotions and work off any irritation you may be feeling. Tinkering with cars or doing carpentry can be very enjoyable, too. You might also be very involved in the lives of your family, perhaps telling them what they should be doing. Your home life is rather fraught at times, especially during heated mealtime discussions.

Mars in the 5th house: creativity

Whenever possible, you really throw yourself into life and like to live it as fully as you can. Sports and athletic activities, or anything else that satisfies your competitive nature, are highly enjoyable although you make it very plain that you don't like being pipped to the winning post. You have a strong desire for activities that give you the scope to express yourself in whichever way comes most naturally. When it comes to love, you enjoy combining a little romance with a lot of sexual passion.

Mars in the 6th house: work and health

Work is an important part of your life, and even if you don't have a job you still need to feel that you're doing something that's worthwhile and helpful. Watch out for a tendency to become a workaholic or to drive yourself on relentlessly until your health is affected. Your relationship with colleagues and employees can be testy at times, especially if you think (or say!) that they don't work hard enough or are too slow. Make sure you find positive ways to burn off excess energy, otherwise your edginess can trigger arguments.

Mars in the 7th house: relationships

You channel a huge amount of emotional energy into your relationships and you expect the same commitment in return. If you don't get what you want, the person concerned soon knows how disappointed you feel. When choosing a partner, you're drawn to someone who is lively, energetic and able to stand up for themselves, and you'll make your move fast before a rival beats you to it. There can be a tendency to squabble with the people in your life, which can create an uncomfortable atmosphere.

Mars in the 8th house: intense emotions

Whether it's with friends, family or a long-term partner, you have a strong drive to establish a close and intense connection with them. Lightweight and inconsequential relationships are a waste of time as far as you're concerned. You need to express your strong sex drive and might enjoy making plenty of conquests. Alternatively, you may renounce sex completely and channel those emotional energies into such profound and mysterious areas as psychology or life after death.

Mars in the 9th house: learning

Adventure, challenges and opportunities always get you buzzing. You're on a constant quest to find more meaning in your life, whether you satisfy that through travel, philosophy, religion, higher education, politics or some other topic that gets you fired up with enthusiasm and reforming zeal. Something to watch out for is a tendency to argue with others over their beliefs in the hope that you'll convert them to your way of thinking. When choosing a partner, they could come from another country or culture.

Mars in the 10th house: reputation

You're highly ambitious and determined to succeed, and you'll do your utmost to make that happen. This gives you tremendous drive and initiative, and it can also mean you're quite prepared to fight your way to success if necessary. However, your relationships may suffer as a result. Beware of giving in to any cut-throat or ruthless tendencies, as these will make you very unpopular and will eventually backfire on you. Disputes with authority figures can also trigger a difficult situation.

Mars in the 11th house: networks

This Mars placing has a strong impact on your friendships, for good or ill. There could be plenty of arguments with friends or you might go into battle for them, perhaps even literally. You often make friends very quickly but they can disappear from your life just as rapidly, especially if you're tempted to boss them around or you get impatient with them once too often. There's also the possibility that a friend could become a lover, or an ex-lover can remain a good friend long after your affair is over.

Mars in the 12th house: retreat

Mars is a very straightforward and direct planet, yet it takes on a confused or secretive flavour in the 12th house. Perhaps you enjoy working behind the scenes, or there may be reasons why you feel unable to step into the spotlight. You have powerful altruistic instincts, so may fight for the underdog or people who are locked away or ignored by society. Sexually, you may be involved in covert relationships that no one must know about, or you might enjoy sexual games played out behind closed doors.

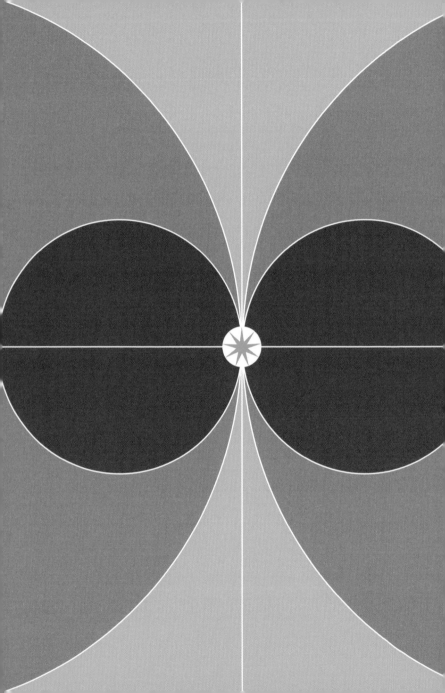

Part five

Love, Sex and Relationships

Venus and Mars are renowned for being a very sexy combination. This part of the book tells you about your own style of loving and sexual expression, according to your Venus and Mars signs. t gives you insights into how your own Venus and Mars get along together, as well as how your Venus hits it off with other people's Mars signs. And, of course, you can read up on your partner's Venus and Mars placings, too, to give you increased insight into what makes them tick in relationships.

Some relationships last and others don't. If you want to know whether a new connection will stand the test of time, this section of the book will give you some valuable pointers based on the position of Venus. You can also discover how to make the first move, according to the sign currently occupied by Mars. And if things don't work out and the time has come to say goodbye, the positions of transiting Venus and Mars can tell you how to do that most effectively.

✳ Venus and your style of loving

The sign occupied by your Venus says a lot about your attitude to love. Does it come naturally to you or does it make you feel slightly uncomfortable? You can also find out about your beloved's Venus sign here.

Natal Venus in Aries

Things happen fast for you, especially when it comes to love and romance. You don't want to waste time, so if you're attracted to someone they'll soon know all about it. The start of a new love affair is always the best bit, as far as you're concerned, and you may even decide that you've never been in love like this before. But will it last? You're easily bored and too much mundane reality can really take the gilt off the romantic gingerbread. You're also much more romantic and idealistic than you like to admit, so it's highly likely that your heart has been broken more than once.

Natal Venus in Taurus

You don't want to be rushed when it comes to your emotions. You're happiest when love grows gradually, stealing up on you a little at a time because if a relationship starts quickly you'll worry that it will end just as fast. Loving relationships, whether they're platonic, sexual or familial, must offer you the emotional security you crave and you'll do your best to give it in return. Although your feelings run deep, try not to be possessive of the people you love. Sex is a vital element in your romantic relationships, especially if it involves plenty of sensual seduction.

Natal Venus in Gemini

As far as you're concerned, love is something to enjoy and to keep you on your toes. Although you can feel deep and sincere emotion, expressing it makes you feel uncomfortable. Instead, you opt for a bright and breezy approach, involving verbal games, repartee and clever conversation. Whenever you fall in love you adore sending letters, cards, texts, emails and little romantic notes to your beloved, and you long for the same in return. If a relationship loses its fizz or becomes predictable, you may decide to look elsewhere for a new love, even if that means two-timing someone.

Natal Venus in Cancer

Love is an essential part of your life and you can't live without it. From an early age you've always needed someone or something to love and care for, whether it's cherished family and friends, a teddy bear or even a houseplant. At times you can be so dependent on other people's affection that you become demanding, needy and reluctant to let them out of your sight. Even so, people love basking in your warmth and kindness because they know that it comes from the heart. A favourite way for you to show your love is by cooking someone a delicious meal or mothering them in some other way.

Natal Venus in Leo

You thrive on the drama and passion of a relationship – the highs, the lows (provided that there aren't too many of them), the arguments and the reconciliations. It's got to keep your interest, so you aren't attracted to anyone who's boring or too timid. You will also avoid anyone who might outshine you in some way unless they do so for reasons that make you swell with pride. A little reflected glory is always welcome! Watch out for any tendencies to tell loved ones what to do. You love making romantic and generous gestures, such as giving lavish presents.

Natal Venus in Virgo

Anyone expecting extravagant displays of emotion – at least in public – will have a long wait. You prefer a much more reticent style, with a dislike of doing anything that might embarrass you. This may mean you come across as uptight and self-conscious sometimes, but it also means that when you do show your feelings there's no doubting their sincerity. Virgo is the sign of the perfectionist, so if you want happy relationships you must learn to curb your tendency to be critical and point out where someone is going wrong. If other areas of your chart agree, you may even be happiest when living alone.

Natal Venus in Libra

It's romance all the way with you. Hearts and flowers, keepsakes and presents, funny little anniversaries, your special song – you simply can't resist all these sentimental reminders of your one true love. However, you get uncomfortable and feel out of your depth if the emotional temperature rises too steeply and the atmosphere gets too intense. This placing gives you an overwhelming need for relationships, sometimes to the point of settling for an arrangement that doesn't make you happy simply because it's preferable to being left on your own.

Natal Venus in Scorpio

Your emotions run so deep that sometimes the only way to handle their intense results, such as jealousy and sexual obsession, is to block them off at their source. Well, you may try to do it, but actually shutting off your feelings may be almost impossible, even if you do manage to bury them most of the time. As a result, you can come across as slightly aloof and remote, even though you're a raging torrent inside. Yet it's essential for your happiness to bond with others, so that you can understand one another and express your rich and deep emotions, ideally at a soul level.

Natal Venus in Sagittarius

You're warm, enthusiastic and affectionate, and thrive on the first flush of excitement that comes with a new love. There's a very idealistic streak to you, making you think that this time things will be different, even if love has disappointed you in the past. You don't like feeling tied down or tethered to anyone's apron strings, and can choose to assert your independence by going off and doing your own thing every now and then. Above all, you want love to be fun and entertaining. You might fall for someone whose culture, background or belief is very different to yours.

Natal Venus in Capricorn

Soft words and sweet nothings aren't your style. They may even send shivers of embarrassment up and down your spine. Even so, you have your own ways of letting someone know that you care about them, although these may be subdued and restrained at times. Loving relationships can hurt you badly when you're young but with age comes experience, as well as happier and more emotionally satisfying encounters. Public displays of affection are a no-no as far as you're concerned because they're not good for your image, but what happens in private is a very different matter.

Natal Venus in Aquarius

There's no doubting your ability to love other people but you aren't always comfortable about showing it. Lavish demonstrations of affection aren't your style – you prefer something much more low-key and controllable. This can disappoint a lover who is expecting a volcano of emotion and can even lead to accusations of being unfeeling or dispassionate. If you fall for someone, you must be able to like them as well as love them, otherwise trouble will brew. Ideally, your partner should be your best friend, so you always have plenty in common even if your sexual relationship goes off the boil.

Natal Venus in Pisces

You have high hopes of love and romance, but does your wish ever come true? For you, love has to be perfect, so you have high ideals and a tendency to put the one you love on a lofty pedestal from which they inevitably fall. It's easy for you to lose yourself in a relationship, and you adore being swept off your feet in that deliciously heady first flush of romance. Settling down into a more predictable routine feels more like hard work, though. There's something effortlessly seductive and attractive about you, even if you aren't aware of it, so you can collect many admirers with no trouble at all.

Mars and your style of sexual expression

How would you define your sexual profile? Are you unrestrained, raunchy, modest or is it such a private area of your life that you feel uncomfortable even thinking about it? The sign occupied by Mars at the time of your birth has a lot to say about your libido and the way you express it.

Natal Mars in Aries

Mars rules Aries, so here's a double helping of Martian haste and urgency. Sex is a vital element in your relationships and may even make or break them. You need a partner who shares your high sex drive and adventurous attitude, otherwise this bedroom mismatch could break your relationship. You make it very plain when you're attracted to someone, possibly even to the point of being blunt or rude, and may find it hard to take the hint if the other person isn't interested. Check your Venus sign. Does it emphasize these characteristics or ameliorate them?

Natal Mars in Taurus

Taurus is a very sensual and physical sign, so a happy and satisfying sex life is essential. You may even ditch someone, despite loving them, because the sexual spark between you is more of a glimmer than a flame, although this is more difficult if you've been together for a long time because of your resistance to the idea of change. You like to take your time when getting to know someone new and won't be hassled into making a commitment. Quick sex isn't your style, either – you want to savour it, like a good meal.

Natal Mars in Gemini

The brain is definitely an erogenous zone for you. Someone might have a pretty or handsome face but their attractions will soon fade if they haven't much between their ears. Witty conversations are a form of foreplay, and even if you're in a committed relationship you still enjoy flirting with other people every now and then. You might even be unfaithful if you get bored with your partner because you hate it when life becomes too predictable. What does a quick fling matter if no one is any the wiser?

Natal Mars in Cancer

If sex isn't accompanied by love, commitment and outpourings of deep emotion, you really aren't interested. Yes, you might have the odd one-night stand but you soon realize that they're not for you. You're hunting for love and stability, so the initial thrill of being treated as a sex object will fizzle out fast if the person doesn't care about you enough. If you want to ask someone out, you take a sideways approach rather than being too direct, and that can lead to crossed wires at times.

Natal Mars in Leo

Sex has got to be glamorous, enjoyable and special. Soft lights, sweet music and maybe some champagne all set the scene for passion, especially if someone wants to seduce you. Sex must also feature you in a starring role, so any partner who ignores your pleasure in favour of their own will either get the cold shoulder or be left behind completely when you move on to someone who appreciates you properly. Ideally, sex should be an act of love, giving you the opportunity to express the warmth and depth of your affections.

Natal Mars in Virgo

This isn't always an easy placing because impetuous and assertive Mars feels hidebound in neat, cautious Virgo. As a result, your sexual expression may not always flow as smoothly as you or your partner would like, especially if you're aware of an inner voice telling you that what you're doing isn't 'nice'. Some with Mars here can find that sex is a horribly messy and embarrassing business, while others love getting up to all sorts of naughty tricks in private. Either way, try not to let your tendency to criticize come between you and your lover.

Natal Mars in Libra

You could be the ideal lover! Sex isn't just about you having a good time – you want to make sure that your partner enjoys themselves as well. This is great if you're with someone who is equally generous but it's ultimately frustrating if they're happy to be the centre of attention while ignoring your needs. You're attracted to people who are intelligent and have interesting things to say for themselves, but they must also be presentable. Sometimes, arguments and spats with your partner are the exciting prelude to passionate sex.

Natal Mars in Scorpio

Sex is a very serious subject for you. Of course, that doesn't mean you can't have a good laugh in the process, but at its best it's a valuable opportunity for you to express your very deep, complex and intense emotions, especially if you normally spend a lot of time trying to keep a lid on them. You need a partner who's as committed to sex as you are, otherwise you'll be deeply frustrated. Sex is also a topic that you consider to be very private and not for general chit-chat. Some people with this placing may decide to abstain from sex completely, often because it's less complicated that way.

Natal Mars in Sagittarius

The more routine or predictable your sex life becomes, the more frustrated you become. You crave adventure and spontaneity, so you need a partner who shares your desire to make sex fun and interesting. They must also be able to laugh at themselves, otherwise their minimal sense of humour will eventually turn you off them. You may take a few risks in order to keep your sex life sizzling and stop it getting stale. It's also vital to have some independence and not be expected to account for every minute of your time when you're away from your partner. Who wants that?

Natal Mars in Capricorn

Appearances can be deceptive! You may give the impression of being conservative, cautious and possibly even rather prim at times, but all that could change when you're with the right person behind closed doors. Or even behind open doors, if that's what you prefer, because this can be a very erotic and sexy placing for Mars. However, even the hottest sexual relationship is called off if the other person embarrasses you once too often. Some people with this placing can sleep with someone because that will help them to get ahead or make some impressive social contacts.

Natal Mars in Aquarius

You don't like playing by the rules or being predictable, so your view of sex can change from one day to the next. It keeps life interesting but it also means that your partner has to be flexible and tolerant, adapting to your tendency to blow hot and cold while trying not to take it personally. The idea of sex by numbers makes you want to forget the whole thing, so you want a partner who shares your inventive and quirky approach. They may also have to accept that occasionally you may stray sexually but it doesn't mean anything to you, although it might do to them.

Natal Mars in Pisces

Sex, when you're with the right person, can be a wonderful means of escape from the drudgery and problems of daily life. Ideally, it should be romantic, otherworldly and seductive. It can even feel like a communion of souls rather than a purely physical act. You're also not averse to a few sexual games, such as role playing, because they appeal to your desire for fantasy. However, you must ensure that these games don't lead you into dangerous situations. You like the idea of fidelity but irresistible temptations can sometimes prevent you putting it into practice.

Venus in Aries combined with Mars

Now we have looked separately at the characteristics of Venus and Mars in your chart, let's combine them and see how that can give us further insights into what love and sex mean to you and how you put that into practice.

Venus in Aries and Mars in Aries

Fiery and lively; argumentative and impulsive; impatient; sexy and flirtatious but not always faithful.

Venus in Aries and Mars in Taurus

Taurus has a steadying influence on Aries; a need for physical contact; affectionate and sensual.

Venus in Aries and Mars in Gemini

Lively, spirited and impatient; flirtatious; always interested in new ideas and activities, so an entertaining companion and inventive in bed.

Venus in Aries and Mars in Cancer

Highly motivated, with a need to get ahead; great for a working partnership; clinginess causes domestic tensions.

Venus in Aries and Mars in Leo

Enthusiastic, fun-loving, demonstrative; playful and affectionate; creative; romantic and loving.

Venus in Aries and Mars in Virgo

Aries impatience and messiness clashes with Virgo perfectionism and neatness; there can be arguments and disputes.

Venus in Aries and Mars in Libra

Balance needed between self-interest and caring for others; relationships are volatile and can be fleeting.

Venus in Aries and Mars in Scorpio

Passionate, intense and highly-charged emotions; strong sexual needs; anger must be expressed, not smothered.

Venus in Aries and Mars in Sagittarius

Entertaining, enterprising, enthusiastic; you enjoy adventures and trying something new; idealistic in love.

Venus in Aries and Mars in Capricorn

Focused, determined, work-orientated; Aries livens up Capricorn; an urge for success and achievement, so relationships may suffer.

Venus in Aries and Mars in Aquarius

A need to be independent; friendly and sociable; good at devising new ideas and plans.

Venus in Aries and Mars in Pisces

Sensitive and easily hurt, despite appearances to the contrary; can have unrealistically high expectations of others.

Venus in Taurus combined with Mars

How does all this come together when you look at your placements of Venus in Taurus and Mars?

Venus in Taurus and Mars in Aries

Easily irritated but slow to get really angry; loving and kind; a need for stability versus desire for excitement.

Venus in Taurus and Mars in Taurus

Tactile, sensual, highly sexed and passionate; laid back and relaxed; must guard against possessiveness.

Venus in Taurus and Mars in Gemini

Easily bored if stuck in an emotional or sexual routine, so may be tempted to stray; may be better as friends than lovers.

Venus in Taurus and Mars in Cancer

A deep need for emotional and physical security; reluctance to embrace chance or take risks; very sensual.

Venus in Taurus and Mars in Leo

Loving, affectionate and kind; considerate towards loved ones; deep reserves of passion.

Venus in Taurus and Mars in Virgo

Grounded, stable and methodical; tendency to stick with whatever is familiar, even if it has lost its sparkle or interest.

Venus in Taurus and Mars in Libra

Dignified on the surface but very sensual and seductive in private; can be reluctant to end a relationship.

Venus in Taurus and Mars in Scorpio

Powerful combination with profound emotional intensity; a deep need for fulfilling sexual expression; earthy and passionate.

Venus in Taurus and Mars in Sagittarius

A complex clash between Taurean need for security and Sagittarian desire for wide open spaces, so can be a partner who sends out mixed messages.

Venus in Taurus and Mars in Capricorn

Strong work ethic and drive; loving but emotionally reserved; deep family values.

Venus in Taurus and Mars in Aquarius

Inner tension, with Taurean emotional needs at odds with Aquarian independence; can be stubborn.

Venus in Taurus and Mars in Pisces

Loving, compassionate and considerate; sensitive and impressionable; supportive in a relationship.

Venus in Gemini combined with Mars

What happens to a Gemini Venus when Mars comes on the scene?

Venus in Gemini and Mars in Aries

Flirty, sociable and friendly; a need to put interesting ideas into practice; can have a relaxed attitude to fidelity.

Venus in Gemini and Mars in Taurus

Easy-going emotions strengthened by earthy desires; possessiveness must be avoided between partners.

Venus in Gemini and Mars in Gemini

Bright, lively, active and eternally youthful; you feel smothered when emotions run high.

Venus in Gemini and Mars in Cancer

Gemini's light touch is given extra meaning by Cancer's care and affection; prone to moodiness.

Venus in Gemini and Mars in Leo

Sociable, entertaining and lively; a strong need to communicate with others and to show deep affection; creative.

Venus in Gemini and Mars in Virgo

Great communication skills; intelligent and analytical; you struggle to express strong emotions in a comfortable way.

Venus in Gemini and Mars in Libra

Articulate, clever and charming; you like to maintain a slightly detached emotional style; you need plenty of wit and repartee.

Venus in Gemini and Mars in Scorpio

Scorpio intensity strengthens or clashes with Gemini's lighter approach; good at business partnerships; you need a partner who makes you think.

Venus in Gemini and Mars in Sagittarius

Fascinated by life and people; great gift for friendship; you love exploring new ideas and interests; not always faithful.

Venus in Gemini and Mars in Capricorn

Rational attitude and emotionally reserved; Gemini's fizz tempered by Capricorn's seriousness.

Venus in Gemini and Mars in Aquarius

Quirky, interesting and intelligent; a strong desire for independence; you enjoy being with kindred spirits; you need a clever partner.

Venus in Gemini and Mars in Pisces

Changeable, fluid and easily bored; can enjoy playing the field but also capable of deep emotion.

Venus in Cancer combined with Mars

If your Venus is in Cancer, how does your Mars affect your attitudes to love and sex?

Venus in Cancer and Mars in Aries

Tenacious and determined; defensive when under pressure; emotional needs clash with desire for independence.

Venus in Cancer and Mars in Taurus

Strong need for emotional and physical security; extremely sensual and affectionate; must have a happy home life.

Venus in Cancer and Mars in Gemini

Yearning for steady emotional life contrasts with urge for variety; you love collecting people and things.

Venus in Cancer and Mars in Cancer

Highly emotional, with deep need for domestic stability and security; moody and sensitive; capable of great passion with the right partner.

Venus in Cancer and Mars in Leo

You enjoy creating a happy home with the focus on family life; caring, affectionate and loyal; you like to be cherished.

Venus in Cancer and Mars in Virgo

Deep emotional needs vie with a no-nonsense attitude; you excel at taking care of others but must let them care for you, too.

Venus in Cancer and Mars in Libra

You love having someone to look after; you need other people and find it hard to end a relationship.

Venus in Cancer and Mars in Scorpio

Highly emotional but will try not to show it; loyal and devoted; can be jealous and defensive.

Venus in Cancer and Mars in Sagittarius

Insecure Cancer is confused by freedom-loving Sagittarius; capable of great insight and understanding; must not get stuck in a sexual rut.

Venus in Cancer and Mars in Capricorn

Powerful urge to create a secure home life; prone to worry, especially about loved ones.

Venus in Cancer and Mars in Aquarius

Uneasy combination of deep emotion and strong rationalism; good at fighting battles for others.

Venus in Cancer and Mars in Pisces

Strongly affected by other people; you pick up on moods and emotional undercurrents; a need to feel loved.

Venus in Leo combined with Mars

If your Venus is in Leo, you can now find out whether sexual sparks will fly when combined with the placement of your Mars.

Venus in Leo and Mars in Aries

Dramatic, lively and energetic; a need for excitement and praise; sociable and outgoing; fiery, sexy and passionate.

Venus in Leo and Mars in Taurus

You need to feel loved and appreciated; you react to necessary change with reluctance and caution; can be stubborn.

Venus in Leo and Mars in Gemini

Bright, interested in life and a great conversationalist; Leo warmth spiced with Gemini wit, making you a lively and entertaining partner.

Venus in Leo and Mars in Cancer

Must have a happy and enriching domestic refuge from the world; strongly focused on family and friends; sex is an important emotional outlet for you.

Venus in Leo and Mars in Leo

Dignified and self-assured; you need a partner to be proud of and who is equally proud of you; loving, demonstrative and obstinate.

Venus in Leo and Mars in Virgo

Leo affection cooled by Virgo self-control; can be very sexy in private; a born organizer.

Venus in Leo and Mars in Libra

Strong need for partnerships and harmonious relationships; affectionate and kind; can be subtly controlling.

Venus in Leo and Mars in Scorpio

Powerfully emotional and intense; a proud and loyal partner; passionate and demonstrative.

Venus in Leo and Mars in Sagittarius

Fun-loving, playful and great sense of humour; interested in exploring the world; optimistic.

Venus in Leo and Mars in Capricorn

Leo warmth tempered by Capricorn reserve; powerful drive for success and achievement; good work partner; can be attracted to somene with status and influence.

Venus in Leo and Mars in Aquarius

You veer between strong affection and a more distant approach; can be dogmatic and intransigent.

Venus in Leo and Mars in Pisces

Loving and demonstrative; idealistic and romantic, so can be disappointed by others; you need a partner who appreciates your creative and artistic talents.

Venus in Virgo combined with Mars

What effect does the placement of your Mars have when your Venus is in Virgo?

Venus in Virgo and Mars in Aries

Virgo modesty and reserve fight with dynamic Aries impulsiveness and urgent sexual needs; if mastered, can lead to a spicy sex life.

Venus in Virgo and Mars in Taurus

Modest and unassuming; quietly loving and faithful; great at getting things done with little fuss.

Venus in Virgo and Mars in Gemini

Brainy and communicative; full of nervous energy; emotional style is slightly detached and withdrawn.

Venus in Virgo and Mars in Cancer

Good at caring for loved ones but a tendency to fuss and nag; the ideal person to help out in a crisis.

Venus in Virgo and Mars in Leo

Loving and attentive; you notice the little things in a relationship; dignified; you worry about welfare of others.

Venus in Virgo and Mars in Virgo

Can be nervy, tense and anxious; fastidious and cautious, but can be sexually unrestrained in private; criticism of loved ones can hurt their feelings.

Venus in Virgo and Mars in Libra

Supportive of partners; can struggle to show your emotions, especially if you think they are irrational or disruptive.

Virgo in Venus and Mars in Scorpio

Strong need to analyse and dissect situations and relationships; can be sexually uninhibited behind closed doors.

Venus in Virgo and Mars in Sagittarius

Inquisitive and interested in other people; partner must be intelligent and good to talk to for a long-lasting relationship.

Venus in Virgo and Mars in Capricorn

Practical, efficient and driven; work and other responsibilities can intrude into the private and family life.

Venus in Virgo and Mars in Aquarius

Emotionally detached and undemonstrative, despite deep feelings; you enjoy debates and arguments.

Venus in Virgo and Mars in Pisces

Sensitive and highly impressionable, so you're tuned into your partner; Virgoan self-control can strengthen Piscean fluid boundaries.

Venus in Libra combined with Mars

With Venus in Libra, what happens when you add a dose of Mars to the equation?

Venus in Libra and Mars in Aries

Libra courtesy clashes with Aries bluntness; you may yearn for a strong relationship but must adapt to your partner's needs.

Venus in Libra and Mars in Taurus

Affectionate, seductive and highly sensual; you enjoy the good things in life; loving and demonstrative.

Venus in Libra and Mars in Gemini

Articulate, charming, diplomatic; you love romance but also need your own space; your partner must be intelligent.

Venus in Libra and Mars in Cancer

Romantic and loving; Libra can be embarrassed by Cancerian sentimentality; surprisingly possessive, which can cause problems.

Venus in Libra and Mars in Leo

Elegant, sophisticated; loving, considerate and romantic; you must have a partner who looks good and knows how to behave.

Venus in Libra and Mars in Virgo

Poise and grace; you need a close relationship but can disrupt it by being too critical.

Venus in Libra and Mars in Libra

Considerate and polite; highly dependent on other people for happiness; you long for a stable relationship.

Venus in Libra and Mars in Scorpio

Libran need for fair play versus Scorpio points-scoring; tumultuous emotions often held in check.

Venus in Libra and Mars in Sagittarius

Easy-going and courteous, but can also be unthinking and brutally honest; partner must have intelligence and wit.

Venus in Libra and Mars in Capricorn

Emotions are carefully expressed because of concern about what others might think, which can lead to emotional restraint.

Venus in Libra and Mars in Aquarius

Deep need for relationships contrasts with desire for independence; you like people who are clever and interesting.

Venus in Libra and Mars in Pisces

Idealistic, romantic and emotionally vulnerable; easily hurt; can shy away from confronting relationship problems and will pretend that all is well.

Venus in Scorpio combined with Mars

Those with Venus in Scorpio can find out here what happens when they add a touch of Mars.

Venus in Scorpio and Mars in Aries

Emotional intensity; tendency to smother disruptive or explosive emotions until they finally erupt in a sexual or furious outburst.

Venus in Scorpio and Mars in Taurus

You experience emotions deeply but struggle to express them; must guard against jealousy or shutting out your partner.

Venus in Scorpio and Mars in Gemini

Your profound Scorpio needs clash with the Gemini desire to keep things light; never a dull moment with the right person.

Venus in Scorpio and Mars in Cancer

You feel deep love and affection; protective of others but trying to control them will lead to problems.

Venus in Scorpio and Mars in Leo

Leo dignity prevents full expression of messy Scorpio feelings; passionate, sexy; can be possessive and bossy.

Venus in Scorpio and Mars in Virgo

Scorpio yearning for deep emotion cooled by Virgo reserve; interested in what makes others tick.

Venus in Scorpio and Mars in Libra

Libra repelled by Scorpio need for high drama and angry scenes; must have a sense of purpose in life; sex can be red hot or stone cold.

Venus in Scorpio and Mars in Scorpio

Powerful both emotionally and sexually; intense feelings that can be difficult to handle so may be blocked out.

Venus in Scorpio and Mars in Sagittarius

Need for emotional intensity contrasts with urge for independence; must have a cause or purpose.

Venus in Scorpio and Mars in Capricorn

Highly motivated and driven; emotions go very deep but aren't easily expressed, which can confuse your partner.

Venus in Scorpio and Mars in Aquarius

Intense and powerful, with strongly held opinions; conflict of emotional interests can lead to confusion in relationships.

Venus in Scorpio and Mars in Pisces

Can be overwhelmed by strong emotions; charismatic and charming; still waters run very deep indeed.

Venus in Sagittarius combined with Mars

Add your Mars placement to your Sagittarian Venus and you get a further layer of understanding.

Venus in Sagittarius and Mars in Aries

Lively, bubbly, full of enthusiasm; flirtatious and impetuous; sometimes you enjoy the thrill of the chase more than the eventual sexual conquest.

Venus in Sagittarius and Mars in Taurus

Carefree emotions held in check by a drive for stability and security; independence versus possessiveness, so you need a partner who understands you.

Venus in Sagittarius and Mars in Gemini

Easy-going, vivacious; you dislike being tied down or feeling trapped; interested in people and in life.

Venus in Sagittarius and Mars in Cancer

A need to be able to wander at will but to return to a safe haven; generous and caring.

Venus in Sagittarius and Mars in Leo

Expansive, dramatic and full of personality; can be hot-tempered, but that adds to the fun when making up afterwards; a great friend and partner.

Venus in Sagittarius and Mars in Virgo

Uneasy blend of Sagittarian relaxation and Virgo perfectionism; interested in ideas, often drawn to a partner's mind over body.

Venus in Sagittarius and Mars in Libra

Intelligent and articulate; warm-hearted and spontaneous; relationships must offer you mental stimulation as well as physical thrills.

Venus in Sagittarius and Mars in Scorpio

You feel things very deeply and can be quick to anger; must search for a spiritual purpose in life and a deep relationship.

Venus in Sagittarius and Mars in Sagittarius

Fun-loving, spontaneous, optimistic; generous; strong desire to explore the world makes for an adventurous partner.

Venus in Sagittarius and Mars in Capricorn

Sagittarian enthusiasms and emotions given depth by Capricorn; can be surprisingly ambitious.

Venus in Sagittarius and Mars in Aquarius

You love intellectual activities; warm and kind; a partner must also be a friend.

Venus in Sagittarius and Mars in Pisces

Idealistic and optimistic; changeable, versatile and easily bored; you love travel and exploring new ideas; sexually adventurous.

Venus in Capricorn combined with Mars

When Capricorn Venus combines with Mars placements, here are the results.

Venus in Capricorn and Mars in Aries

Hard-working, motivated; can sacrifice love for ambition; strong sexual desires behind closed doors.

Venus in Capricorn and Mars in Taurus

Emotionally reserved but feelings go deep; must guard against being possessive or materialistic.

Venus in Capricorn and Mars in Gemini

Wry wit and a slight air of detachment; embarrassed by big displays of emotion.

Venus in Capricorn and Mars in Cancer

Reticent about showing emotions and you try to hide deep feelings; strong family bonds are essential.

Venus in Capricorn and Mars in Leo

Dignified and self-assured; concerned about having a good image; quietly supportive and loving.

Venus in Capricorn and Mars in Virgo

Shy, reserved; scared of being hurt emotionally so can favour logic and facts over feelings.

Venus in Capricorn and Mars in Libra

Focused, dependable, hard-working; you want to create a good impression and earn the respect of others; you're a very supportive partner.

Venus in Capricorn and Mars in Scorpio

Quiet, serious; a cauldron of deep emotion simmers beneath a cool and calm exterior; you're hot stuff in private.

Venus in Capricorn and Mars in Sagittarius

You feel uncomfortable being demonstrative but must express your Sagittarian warmth.

Venus in Capricorn and Mars in Capricorn

Feelings held in check; dislike of overt emotional displays; quietly affectionate and kind.

Venus in Capricorn and Mars in Aquarius

Rational; you take life and love seriously; reserved and undemonstrative; you need room to breathe.

Venus in Capricorn and Mars in Pisces

Torn between being withdrawn and cautious, and being more open and affectionate; logic versus instincts.

Venus in Aquarius combined with Mars

When Venus is in Aquarius, interpreting your Mars placement can tell you a lot about your style of loving.

Venus in Aquarius and Mars in Aries

Independent, free-wheeling; Aquarian detachment contrasts with Aries enthusiasm and affection.

Venus in Aquarius and Mars in Taurus

Loyal and reliable; a staunch friend; can be stubborn and intransigent; you honour solid and heartfelt values.

Venus in Aquarius and Mars in Gemini

Clever, astute; you love communicating with others; uncomfortable during big emotional scenes.

Venus in Aquarius and Mars in Cancer

Awkward combination of Aquarian independence and Cancerian neediness; desire to mother the world, which may trigger a partner's possessiveness or jealousy.

Venus in Aquarius and Mars in Leo

Warm and friendly but you struggle to be openly demonstrative; must be proud of your partner.

Venus in Aquarius and Mars in Virgo

A need to create emotional distance from others at times; friendly and supportive, but can be dispassionate.

Venus in Aquarius and Mars in Libra

Clever and good conversationalist; torn between slight emotional aloofness and a desire to create harmony in all your relationships.

Venus in Aquarius and Mars in Scorpio

You dislike letting others under your emotional radar; a need to maintain barriers and boundaries; obstinate.

Venus in Aquarius and Mars in Sagittarius

Friendly, outgoing, sociable; a need for emotional freedom rather than being hampered by demands of others.

Venus in Aquarius and Mars in Capricorn

Great at dealing with practicalities and ideas but can struggle to express your emotions.

Venus in Aquarius and Mars in Aquarius

Can be emotionally self-sufficient; may be more comfortable with friendships than messy relationships.

Venus in Aquarius and Mars in Pisces

Dispassionate Aquarius softened by sensitive Pisces; powerful humanitarian instincts and drives.

Venus in Pisces combined with Mars

What happens when you combine Venus in Pisces with your Mars placement?

Venus in Pisces and Mars in Aries

Vulnerable Pisces backed up by Aries strength and determination; can be confused by your emotions.

Venus in Pisces and Mars in Taurus

Deep need for emotional security and reliability; warm, loving and affectionate; family-minded.

Venus in Pisces and Mars in Gemini

Impressionable, inventive, changeable; partners and friends must appeal at an emotional and intellectual level.

Venus in Pisces and Mars in Cancer

Can become defensive when swamped by emotions; kind, caring, loving; you need someone to look after or dote on.

Venus in Pisces and Mars in Leo

Immensely creative and artistic; strong desire for self-expression; longing for glamour and excitement in relationships.

Venus in Pisces and Mars in Virgo

Potential clash between fluid emotions and practical desires; high expectations; can enjoy rescuing others.

Venus in Pisces and Mars in Libra

Romantic idealism can lead to dashed hopes; love life must be perfect; affectionate; you avoid upsetting or difficult scenes.

Venus in Pisces and Mars in Scorpio

Deep emotions and drives that can be hard to express or manage; you want relationships that really mean something.

Venus in Pisces and Mars in Sagittarius

Versatile, mutable, swiftly bored; can learn a lot from relationships; easily consumed and led by emotion.

Venus in Pisces and Mars in Capricorn

Pisces sensitivity and vulnerability blended with Capricorn common sense; must have a dependable partner.

Venus in Pisces and Mars in Aquarius

Swirling Piscean emotions given structure by rational Aquarius; gift for friendship; you need to take care of others.

Venus in Pisces and Mars in Pisces

May struggle to deal with ever-changing or overwhelming emotions; idealistic, romantic, escapist.

Who do you love?

Your natal Venus has plenty to say about the sort of person you love, whether they're your partner, friend or a member of your family. And, of course, you can find out someone's Venus sign to see what they're looking for in you.

Natal Venus in Aries

Apart from yourself, you love anyone who's fun-loving, spontaneous and has a streak of daring and impetuosity. Anyone who's too predictable or boring will never get far with you. You're also turned off by meanness and petty-mindedness, regardless of who's doing the penny-pinching.

Natal Venus in Taurus

Oh, for someone who is dependable, reliable and loyal! You need to know you can count on people because there's always the risk that anyone who's too fly-by-night could let you down. You yearn for staunch friends, loving relatives, friendly colleagues and a partner who's passionate and sexy.

Natal Venus in Gemini

Potential lovers and friends must have one thing in common – brains. You're just as easily seduced by someone's words and thoughts as by their looks or actions. You need a partner who appreciates you and doesn't want to change you, and who doesn't mind you flirting with other people every now and then.

Natal Venus in Cancer

You're drawn to people who are affectionate and kind, or who you suspect are in need of some tender loving care so you can wrap them in your particular style of affection, like a warm blanket. You feel uneasy and guarded when you're with anyone who's blunt or too emotionally remote.

Natal Venus in Leo

Deep down, you believe that someone has to be worthy of your love before you'll give it wholeheartedly. Once you do give your heart, you're loyal, supportive and encouraging. You're drawn towards people who are creative, entertaining and affectionate. You like being proud of loved ones.

Natal Venus in Virgo

Anyone who is good at what they do gets your vote every time. They also need to be tidy, clean and presentable, and also to be helpful. People who can encourage you to open up emotionally are good for you because they teach you to let your feelings flow rather than to continually analyse them.

Natal Venus in Libra

If someone is going to win your friendship or your heart they must be clever, articulate, well-mannered and easy on the eye. They must have brains as well as beauty, otherwise you're quickly bored. You also need to be with people who appreciate how sensitive and easily hurt you can be.

Natal Venus in Scorpio

You have no interest in anyone who is superficial or who flits from one relationship to the next. Instead, you're looking for commitment, purpose and loyalty, and you'll stick like glue when you find someone with these qualities. Your partner must know how to weather your dramatic emotional storms.

Natal Venus in Sagittarius

Someone's social or financial standing means nothing to you. What does appeal is their brain. Are they interesting to talk to? Do they get you thinking? And, most importantly, do they understand you? Your ideal partner must be clever, entertaining, positive and encouraging.

Natal Venus in Capricorn

Some people with this placing will marry for money or power. Even if that's a step too far, anyone you're attracted to must have some element of respectability or status. They must also be sensible, mature and quietly sexy, and it definitely helps if they share your dry sense of humour.

Natal Venus in Aquarius

It's almost impossible for you to fall for someone you don't like, so friends can become lovers and lovers, when the initial passion has faded, can become friends. Any important person in your life must also be intelligent, witty and worth talking to, otherwise you simply can't be bothered with them.

Natal Venus in Pisces

Anyone you love must be kind, considerate and nice to be around. Ideally, they should also be easy on the eye, especially if you have romantic designs on them. If you have strong beliefs, such as spiritual values, you'll enjoy sharing those ideas with friends, family and lovers.

Making the first move

Letting someone know you're interested in them, or making the first move, can be daunting. Tune into the energy of the current Mars sign so you know what to do and – just as importantly – what not to do. Find out where Mars is in the zodiac right now by referring to the back of the book, an astrology program, app or website, then look up that sign here.

When Mars is in Aries

Boom! You feel almost irresistible red-hot attraction and desire, and you're desperate to act on it. Try not to be too pushy and insistent, in case the other person isn't as keen on you as you are on them. This could turn out to be a quick fling rather than a long-term relationship.

When Mars is in Taurus

This isn't a good time for spur-of-the-moment decisions – you want to take things slowly so you can be sure of your ground. When arranging a date, opt for a romantic and sensual setting, such as a luxurious picnic in a private outdoor spot or a delicious candlelit dinner.

When Mars is in Gemini

Someone's conversation or intelligence could be a bigger turn-on than their appearance right now. Flirtatious and witty conversations, emails and texts give you a buzz and might lead to sex but not necessarily to a new long-term relationship. Is it just a bit of temporary fun?

When Mars is in Cancer

Even if you're normally very straightforward you may find that you're tongue-tied or indirect when asking someone out. Delicious food is a must-have when choosing the venue for a first date, and ideally it should be in a traditional or historic setting, too.

When Mars is in Leo

You need to keep your dignity when chatting someone up or asking them out. Suggest doing something that involves a little luxury, such as a meal in the best restaurant you can afford. Avoid any moves that shout 'cheapskate'. This isn't the time to be miserly.

When Mars is in Virgo

This is ideal for getting together with a colleague or someone else you've met through work. However, it could be hard to summon up the courage to make that all-important first move for fear of being rejected or made to feel foolish. Take it small step by small step.

When Mars is in Libra

Don't be surprised if you're in two minds about whether to make a move on someone. It's a typical case of Libran indecision. If you do ask someone out, make sure that you're looking good and suggest a venue for your date that is elegant and pleasant, not rough and ready.

When Mars is in Scorpio

There could be a lot of careful forethought and planning before you gear yourself up to ask someone out. Try not to second-guess the outcome or become suspicious – or furious – if you don't get the response you wanted. Chalk it up to experience and move on.

When Mars is in Sagittarius

Just do it! This isn't a time for caution or playing safe. You may even find that you've blurted out what you wanted to say almost without being aware of it. Suggest a date that's interesting and most definitely not boring or predictable, such as a meal in an exotic restaurant.

When Mars is in Capricorn

Dare you do it or will you be rejected? Try not to let fear stand in the way if you want to ask someone out because you might be pleasantly surprised when they say 'yes'. Choose a venue for your date that's classic or impressive while keeping the atmosphere relaxed and easy.

When Mars is in Aquarius

You may meet through a mutual friend. If you're looking for a way of breaking the ice, find a goal or interest that you have in common. This isn't the right time to come on too strong, so you need to play it cool without being so chilly that the other person thinks you don't like them.

When Mars is in Pisces

Don't let shyness or lack of confidence hold you back from making the first move. This is a great phase for little romantic gestures and acts of kindness. An ideal date could be a trip to the cinema or ballet, going dancing, a visit to an art gallery or a candlelit dinner.

Love, sweet love

Looking at the astrology of the moment when you meet someone new, or when a relationship really clicks, will tell you a lot about what's going on. The sign occupied by Venus at the time will give you strong hints about the type of love or friendship you can expect. Simply look in the back of the book, or online to find the sign that Venus is moving through – or transiting.

When Venus is in Aries

Everything happens fast. You might meet for coffee one day and be living together the next. Whether it's romance or a friendship, it's going to be interesting and upbeat, but don't let too much idealism about how things should be get in the way of how things really are.

When Venus is in Taurus

This is going to be a relationship that's all about quiet and contented emotional bonds. You'll want to establish a deep connection with one another, but don't expect it to happen overnight. Slow but sure wins this particular race. Watch out for signs of potential possessiveness, though.

When Venus is in Gemini

Any relationship that begins under this placing is going to involve a lot of chatter. You'll have so much to say to one another, including catching up on the latest gossip, whether face to face, on the phone or online. Going off on short jaunts, such as day trips or shopping sprees, is also likely.

When Venus is in Cancer

Don't be surprised if the two of you spend a lot of time eating, cooking and generally being cosy. If you move in together, your home will feel like a safe haven against the world. Family is an important element of your relationship, whether it consists of children or pets.

When Venus is in Leo

Get ready for drama, excitement and grand gestures. This relationship will feel special and vibrant, regardless of whether it's passionate or platonic. It could also work out expensive, thanks to visits to the theatre and high-end restaurants, and exchanging lots of luxurious presents.

When Venus is in Virgo

This is a classic placing for meeting a new friend or even your one true love through work or an activity connected with health. Things may get off to a slow start and there may always be a slight air of reserve and shyness between you. Even so, a sexual relationship could be dynamite.

When Venus is in Libra

The emphasis is on togetherness, so you could get very starry-eyed if you meet someone new. This might be the start of a wonderful romance, but there's also the chance of wanting it to succeed so much that you both turn a blind eye to each other's faults in a haze of idealistic dreams.

When Venus is in Scorpio

Any relationship that begins under Venus in Scorpio will be strong, complex and dramatic. It also stands a good chance of lasting, and this is certainly a great time to make a deep emotional commitment to someone. You know that life will never be quite the same again.

When Venus is in Sagittarius

There will be plenty to talk about, and possibly to disagree about, too. You may have met in a bookshop, library or exotic restaurant, or while travelling. This is a relationship that thrives on space and independence, with an emphasis on adapting to one another's needs and interests.

When Venus is in Capricorn

You might meet at work or through some other form of business contact, and your relationship may always feel serious and significant. This is a partnership that's slightly restrained, formal and low-key on the surface, even if you're staunch and supportive partners for life.

When Venus is in Aquarius

Friendship is bound to play a big role in your relationship – you might meet through joint friends or start off as chums. Whatever the nature of your relationship, it will have a strongly independent streak. It might also have an element of controversy or shock that always gets people talking.

When Venus is in Pisces

This relationship could start for reasons connected with alcohol, perfume, fishing, music or dance. You might even meet through a charity or some other humanitarian project. The bond between you will always have a slightly mysterious or elusive quality, or could be muddled in some way.

✳✳ Saying
✳✳ goodbye
✳✳

Some relationships last a lifetime, others come and go. The transiting positions of Venus and Mars – the zodiac signs they are passing through at the time – will give you vital clues about what to expect, the reasons for the problems and whether breaking up will be hard to do.

When Venus is in Aries

There could be a few fireworks, especially if you're the one who's initiating the break-up and the other person gets defensive. Alternatively, everything could come to an end because one or both of you feels bored and wants to move on to pastures new.

When Venus is in Taurus

It's never easy to break up when Venus is in Taurus because this is a placing that needs stability. It might be better to wait until Venus moves into Gemini. Problems connected with possessiveness, stubbornness or money could trigger the end of the relationship.

When Venus is in Gemini

If you need to say farewell to someone, you'll find it easy to do so with a light touch. This is also a good time to say your goodbyes with the help of a carefully worded letter, but definitely not a text! Flirtatiousness, boredom or infidelity could be the cause of the break-up.

When Venus is in Cancer

This isn't a good time to sever your ties with someone. Venus in Cancer is all about staying together, even if it would be better if you were apart. Resist the temptation to give a doomed relationship another try just for old times' sake. Smother-love could be the final straw.

When Venus is in Leo

If you're the one saying goodbye you must try to protect the other person's pride and self-respect. Let them down gently but honestly, and throw in a few compliments to soothe their battered ego. Issues around control and bossiness are likely to loom large.

When Venus is in Virgo

Getting up the nerve to bid someone farewell could be the big stumbling block. You don't want to appear rude and you'll work hard to save the other person's feelings. Problems connected with someone being overly critical, faddy or uptight could push things to breaking point.

When Venus is in Libra

This placing is all about being polite and part of a team, so it's not great for splitting up. You may worry about being left on the shelf or getting drawn into a row, even to the point of deciding that it's easier to stay together. Someone's exaggerated desire to please may drive you apart.

When Venus is in Scorpio

Emotions are potent and highly charged, so breaking up will be a powerful experience that you won't forget in a hurry, no matter how much you'd like to. Resist the temptation to get bogged down in recriminations. Clashes over jealousy or sex could be a deal-breaker.

When Venus is in Sagittarius

Whoever wants to end the relationship will see it from a philosophical angle and insist that it's no big deal. This is a good placing for a civilized parting of the ways, with strong ideals about how to behave. Disagreements about your opinions or beliefs might be the main problem.

When Venus is in Capricorn

Expressing your true feelings will be hard because of an atmosphere of emotional restraint. Your parting will feel chilly and reserved. Problems about goals, responsibilities and work will come up.

When Venus is in Aquarius

This Venus sign brings a friendly but remote parting of the ways, with strong ideals about the need to behave and respect one another. There's an emphasis on remaining friends. Disputes about someone's obstinacy, their need to be right or their social life could finally drive you apart.

When Venus is in Pisces

The last thing you'll want to do is cause upset or hurt feelings, so you'll have to steel yourself to say what's necessary or wait until Venus moves into Aries. Don't over-romanticize your relationship or make it a long drawn-out goodbye. Issues about trust, reality and escapism may be the final straw.

When Mars is in Aries

Expect some drama! A Mars in Aries break-up involves noisy rows and possibly even some slammed doors, so avoid this phase if you don't want to get embroiled in big scenes. Relationship problems will revolve around someone's bad temper, selfishness or rash decisions.

When Mars is in Taurus

There's a reluctance to change the status quo, so you may feel bogged down and stuck. Try not to adopt an uncompromising and entrenched attitude because being obstinate won't help the situation. Difficulties about money, materialism and jealousy can loom large.

When Mars is in Gemini

This is good for arguing your case and saying what you think, but watch out for sharp words, sarcasm and verbal battles. You may say something in the heat of the moment that you regret later on. Arguments focus on bickering, flirtatiousness and clashes of opinion.

When Mars is in Cancer

Complaints and comments are met with defensiveness and huffiness, which can make it hard to get your point across. One of you may be determined to cling on to the relationship, even if it should have ended long ago. Disputes are connected with family matters, domesticity and clinginess.

When Mars is in Leo

Tread softly, for you tread on someone's ego. Denting their self-esteem by breaking up with them could lead to major tantrums, so you must let them down gently. Arguments that crop up at this time will centre on bossiness, jealousy and wanting to be in charge.

When Mars is in Virgo

If you're thinking of ending a relationship, you need to plan ahead. Work out what to say and how to say it, so you'll have the confidence to go through with your plans. Disagreements when Mars is in Virgo focus on honouring commitments, working too hard and untidiness.

When Mars is in Libra

It's essential to play fair and be considerate, especially if you're going to end a relationship. Don't be surprised if you have second thoughts about breaking up or find it harder than you imagined. Disputes that come with Mars in Libra are about injustice and rudeness.

When Mars is in Scorpio

This is a difficult placing because of its high-voltage intensity and simmering emotions. Don't say or do anything that will provoke unnecessary anger or unpleasant scenes, and be prepared to hear some home truths. Rows that crop up will be about jealousy, recriminations and sex.

When Mars is in Sagittarius

The urge for freedom is very strong when Mars is in Sagittarius, so it might be a good time to part company from someone. Watch out for angry conversations and don't use words as weapons. Arguments will revolve around politics, differing viewpoints and honesty.

When Mars is in Capricorn

Breaking up with someone may be an oddly dispassionate and clinical experience. There's an emphasis on doing things properly, working out who owns what and possibly also worries about what others will say. Rows will be about ambition, determination and materialism.

When Mars is in Aquarius

This is a good time to let someone go their own way, especially if you have differing ideals and dreams. Try not to get drawn into discussions about what each of you should have done and where you've gone wrong. Disputes will be about change for its own sake and wanting to rebel.

When Mars is in Pisces

Feeling angry is one thing but expressing it is quite another. Your fury may fizzle out, leaving you frustrated and unable to say what's wrong. There can be a feeling of unfinished business if you part from someone. Disagreements will be about deceit, playing the victim, addiction or never being available.

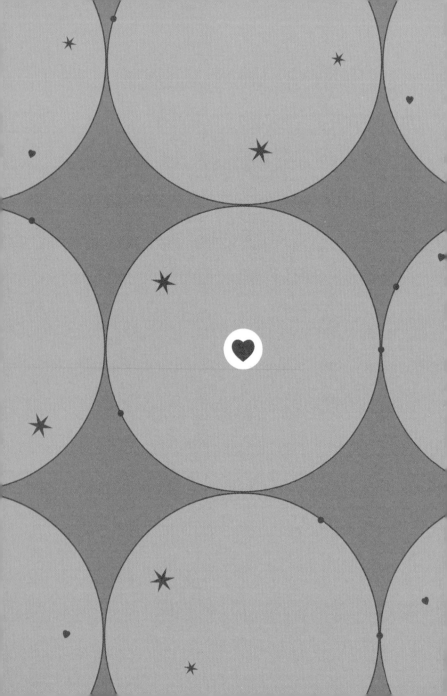

Part six

Playing to Your Strengths

Every sign has its good and bad points, but in this section of the book we're concentrating firmly on making the most of each sign's strengths. You'll learn how the sign occupied by your Venus will help you to discover your heart's desire, and how your Mars sign will reveal what you want out of life. This section will also tell you how your Venus and Mars signs reveal what you're like at work, as well as what makes you angry and how to keep the peace.

You can take all this one step further by considering other areas of your life and combining them with the meanings of your Venus and Mars signs. Use your knowledge of yourself as a starting point and think about previous triumphs. What do they say about your Venus and Mars signs, and how can you build on them in the future? You'll find that there are many ways to play to your strengths.

✳ Finding your heart's desire

If your fairy godmother waved a magic wand and said that you could have anything your heart desired, what would you choose? The sign occupied by your natal Venus will give you some clues about what you yearn for in life.

Natal Venus in Aries

You long for excitement and drama. Life for you has to be a rollercoaster ride, but with the chance to get off every now and then so you can catch your breath. In material terms, you love anything that gives you a thrill, such as a fast car or something mechanical and slightly dangerous.

Natal Venus in Taurus

You dream of leading a simple, uncomplicated life. You need your creature comforts, of course, but nothing too fancy. Being surrounded by nature, tending your own garden, enjoying the company of loved ones and having enough money will all help you to connect with your heart's desire.

Natal Venus in Gemini

For you, it's all about being interested in life. You enjoy feeling that you're never quite sure what's around the corner. You love meeting new people and communicating with others always gives you a buzz. You also adore the idea of meeting your twin soul, whoever they are.

Natal Venus in Cancer

Emotional security is your number one priority. This can come in many different forms, provided that it makes you feel warm and cosy inside. You're instinctively maternal, regardless of your gender, with a profound need to be able to take care of others and to have a happy home life.

Natal Venus in Leo

You long for creative outlets for your energies and talents, because without them you feel stifled and frustrated. It's vital for you to be able to express your true self, and to enjoy yourself in the process. Your romantic soul also yearns for the opportunity to love and to be loved in return.

Natal Venus in Virgo

Whatever your age or job status, you need to feel useful. You love helping others, especially in health matters, and you will gladly do all sorts of little chores for them, too. You take pleasure in details, so might enjoy working on fiddly or small things, such as making dolls' clothes or jewellery.

Natal Venus in Libra

Having someone in your life who you truly care about is an absolute necessity, especially if they're your romantic equal. It's very difficult for you to feel happy and fulfilled if you're on your own, so if you don't have a partner you'll want to forge strong bonds with friends or family instead.

Natal Venus in Scorpio

Intensity. It's what you live for. You need to get an emotional charge out of almost everything you do, otherwise life starts to lose its purpose. At its very best, love offers you the chance of some kind of transformation. This can translate into a series of powerful emotional encounters.

Natal Venus in Sagittarius

You're always searching for the next goal or experience. Travel, whether of the mind, body or spirit, is an essential part of your life, giving it meaning and purpose. You love books, adventures and interesting companions, but most of all you love and need the concept of hope.

Natal Venus in Capricorn

You need to feel that you've achieved something worthwhile in life. This might be material or emotional, but it must matter to you and give you a sense of purpose. Your achievements must also be recognized by others, because you need their approval and admiration.

Natal Venus in Aquarius

Being allowed to be yourself and being accepted for who you are – these are essential requirements for you. Your innate honesty will never let you pretend to be something you're not, and you'll delight in creating a few shockwaves if you feel the conversation is getting too staid or conventional.

Natal Venus in Pisces

Losing yourself in something bigger than you, such as a relationship, vocation, creative activity or spiritual pursuit, is one of your biggest dreams. It helps you to feel a greater connection with the rest of the world or, sometimes, another and more perfect world.

What do you want?

'I want' is a classic Mars phrase. But what does your Mars want? Check your sign to discover what you desire from life and how you might be able to get it.

Natal Mars in Aries

Thrills, exhilaration, fun and a little danger all give you a buzz. Without them, life feels drab, grey and energy-sapping. Something else you want is independence and the ability to show off your leadership skills, both at work and in your private life.

Natal Mars in Taurus

Stability and loyalty are everything to you. You must know where you stand, both emotionally and materially. Your wishlist includes having (more than) enough money in the bank, a dependable but sexy partner and enjoying a stable home life.

Natal Mars in Gemini

You're looking for an interesting life with plenty of variety so there's little danger of you getting bored or stale. Ideas excite you and you enjoy discussing them, provided that you have the last word, of course. You also want to keep on the move so are never in one place for long.

Natal Mars in Cancer

A happy and fulfilling home life is a huge objective for you, and when you've got it you'll hold on to it come what may. Your home is your refuge from the rest of the world. You want to provide for your family, not only materially but emotionally, too.

Natal Mars in Leo

Activities that allow you to express yourself are essential to your happiness, and frustration follows if your creative drive is blocked for some reason. It doesn't suit you to keep yourself small and insignificant. You have a huge urge for a loving family and close friends.

Natal Mars in Virgo

It's very simple – you want to be of service. That might be through your work or in your spare time, but you must feel that you're helping out in some way. This can lead to always being on call, so avoid that by making sure that you have strong boundaries.

Natal Mars in Libra

You want to forge a feeling of togetherness and partnership with other people. Being solo for long doesn't suit you, and ideally you need to share your life with a long-term partner. If that isn't possible, you must be able to bond with good friends or family.

Natal Mars in Scorpio

Rather like a mathematical formula, the effort that you put into something must be matched by the satisfaction it gives you. This applies in every area of your life but especially in relationships. Take care that this doesn't lead to obsessiveness or jealousy.

Natal Mars in Sagittarius

It's essential for you to have targets in life that you can aim at. Sometimes you hit them, sometimes you don't, but the fun lies in trying your luck. You can't resist a good challenge, and you also feel that you must stand up for what you believe in.

Natal Mars in Capricorn

You want the three Rs: respect, recognition and reputation. These can come with the fourth R of responsibility, which is fine by you because you're so conscientious. You aren't afraid of hard work, especially if it will bring you that all-important status and success.

Natal Mars in Aquarius

It's easy. You want a life full of freedom, independence and originality, so you can truly be yourself, without the obligation to follow anyone else's rules. You may raise a few eyebrows or break conventions but hey, who cares? You certainly don't!

Natal Mars in Pisces

Very often, and especially whenever life gets tough or unpleasant, you want to escape into a nicer world. You might do this by turning off your phone, avoiding certain people or indulging in alcohol, drugs or sex. Something else that you want is to help others or even rescue them.

Venus at work

What sort of colleague are you? Do you like to feel you're part of a team or do you prefer to be a solo act? The sign of your natal Venus describes the working atmosphere that suits you best.

Natal Venus in Aries

You don't like working alone for too long. You need the stimulus and buzz of other people, provided that they're lively, good fun and intelligent. The atmosphere must be fast-paced and busy, and even if you're at the bottom of the pecking order you'll want to take the initiative at times.

Natal Venus in Taurus

It's good to have some friendly colleagues, especially if they don't expect you to be a workaholic. Edible treats play a big role in your working routine, so you'll suggest taking it in turns to provide home-baked goodies, but woe betide anyone who doesn't contribute!

Natal Venus in Gemini

You need to be part of a team, whether it's big or small. Working by yourself won't suit you because you thrive on bouncing ideas off other people, and who will you gossip with if it's only you in the room? You may also be the office mimic, perfectly capturing everyone's idiosyncrasies.

Natal Venus in Cancer

Wherever you work, it must have the right atmosphere or you'll feel uncomfortable. Ideally, you should be with friendly colleagues rather than on your own, so you can bond with them. If anyone is having a tough time, they'll instinctively turn to you and you'll do your best to help.

Natal Venus in Leo

It's quite likely that you're one of the most popular people at work. Colleagues enjoy your creative input, emotional warmth and encouragement, but may not be so keen when you're being bossy or egotistical. You love organizing office junkets and outings.

Natal Venus in Virgo

You're far too modest to blow your own trumpet but you take pride in doing your very best at work. That means doing your job as well as possible, and maybe even developing new systems and routines while wondering why your colleagues can't follow suit.

Natal Venus in Libra

This is the placing of the peacemaker, so your role at work is often to intercede whenever trouble brews between colleagues and to calm things down. You may even work as an agent or negotiator, which gives you plenty of scope to demonstrate your diplomatic skills.

Natal Venus in Scorpio

You must put a tremendous amount of emotional energy into your work or you can't see any point in doing it. Working alone suits you, but this must be balanced by time spent with others. Colleagues have to pull their weight, otherwise you'll let them know what you think of them.

Natal Venus in Sagittarius

Although you may enjoy working alone for a while, ultimately you need to have people around you to chat with and stop you getting bored. You're a great colleague, full of fun and encouragement, but you also enjoy being self-employed. Your ideal job involves teaching, books or travel.

Natal Venus in Capricorn

You enjoy showing what you're capable of, and it gives you great pleasure to get pats on the back and recognition for all your efforts. You're a trustworthy member of the team and are delighted if you're asked to step into a position of power or authority.

Natal Venus in Aquarius

You have the best of both worlds because you're a fabulous team member and you also enjoy working on your own or being self-employed. You're not great at taking orders, especially if they're from someone who doesn't do their job nearly as well as you do yours.

Natal Venus in Pisces

Whether you work alone or in a group, you must feel that you're doing something worthwhile and rewarding. And if you can help someone, so much the better. A dead-end job or unpleasant colleagues will soon sap your energy, and you'll find all sorts of reasons to make yourself scarce.

Mars at work

This is the planet that describes your drive and determination, so what does the position of Mars in your birth chart – your natal Mars – say about your behaviour at work? Do you like to be in charge or do you prefer to let others take the helm?

Natal Mars in Aries

Regardless of your job, you must have some autonomy because being told what to do will eventually infuriate you. You're great at getting projects off the ground but are much less interested in finishing them. Colleagues can be competitors and sparring partners.

Natal Mars in Taurus

If the world is divided into tortoises and hares, you're definitely a tortoise. You take your time and refuse to be rushed, so a hectic or pressured environment may not suit you. You're happy to be given instructions but find it difficult to be adaptable or to change your mind.

Natal Mars in Gemini

Whatever you do for a living, it must involve contact with other people so you can bounce ideas off them, chat to them and be inspired by them when necessary. You're at your best when hatching plans and coming up with brilliant solutions to seemingly insoluble problems.

Natal Mars in Cancer

Your innate ambition powers you through your working life, and you'll happily put in the hours to get ahead. You love working from home, provided that you can avoid the inevitable distractions. If you share a workspace, you can't resist mothering your colleagues.

Natal Mars in Leo

Even if you're at the bottom of the pecking order at work, you must have some form of authority otherwise you lose interest. You're happiest when you're the one in charge, so you can exercise your organizational skills, but beware of becoming too bossy or condescending.

Natal Mars in Virgo

You're a very willing worker. The idea of shirking or not doing your duty doesn't even enter your head, so you're the one who's still at work long after your colleagues have gone home. Watch out for workaholic tendencies that could eventually affect your health.

Natal Mars in Libra

You have a strong need to be successful. If your job involves diplomacy, mediation or the law, then you're on exactly the right track because these are areas where you excel. It's important to have an attractive working space and amenable colleagues.

Natal Mars in Scorpio

Productive and hard-working, you always put plenty of effort into your job. Sometimes you might even put in so much effort that it's almost impossible to switch off and relax. You need some element of control and autonomy, otherwise you'll get very frustrated.

Natal Mars in Sagittarius

With your love of a challenge and opportunity, the last thing you want is a tedious or mind-numbing job. You must find worthy channels for your enthusiasm, branching out, trying new ideas and pushing yourself, otherwise you could become slapdash.

Natal Mars in Capricorn

You don't mind starting at the bottom rung of the career ladder if necessary but you certainly won't stay there for long. You'll work hard to climb the greasy pole of success, putting in extra hours or hobnobbing with influential contacts in order to make it in life.

Natal Mars in Aquarius

Work must offer you the chance to demonstrate your initiative and ingenuity, preferably without having to justify your actions to anyone else. Self-employment suits you, provided that someone else keeps on top of all the tedious paperwork. Colleagues must also be friends.

Natal Mars in Pisces

You want a job or vocation that captures your imagination and calls to you emotionally, otherwise you'll resent it. Ideally, it should draw on your creative talents, too. Charity work, or helping people who are ignored by or hidden from society, could also appeal.

Your powers of attraction

It's no coincidence that the symbol for Venus looks like a hand-held mirror because this planet is concerned with appearances and looking good. How can you make the most of the position of Venus in your birth chart?

Natal Venus in Aries

It's very important for you to look good. That's partly because you can't help checking your reflection in the nearest mirror but also because you adore receiving compliments. Aries rules the head, so you need to draw attention to this part of your body, whether with hats, amazing glasses or a dramatic hairstyle.

Natal Venus in Taurus

If it doesn't feel right or smell nice, you aren't bothered. You're drawn to fabrics and scents that are natural, so manmade fibres and synthetic-smelling perfumes are a no-no. The throat is ruled by Taurus and you love making the most of yours with attractive scarves, collars and jewellery.

Natal Venus in Gemini

Do you look your age? It's highly unlikely! You'll look young throughout your life and your wardrobe is never stuck in a rut either. You love combining separates in all sorts of inventive ways, and have a weakness for bangles, bracelets and rings that complement your attractive hands.

Natal Venus in Cancer

The lure of the past gets you every time, so some of your clothes may be old friends you've had for ages or vintage finds that give you a distinctive image. Anything that's too contemporary or cutting edge is likely to repel you because it isn't familiar enough. You love snuggling into woollen garments.

Natal Venus in Leo

This is one of the most glamorous placings for Venus. Looking fabulous is essential for you, with flattering clothes that appear expensive, even if they aren't, and hair that's glossy and beautifully cut. After all, you have an image to maintain and you never ever want to look less than your best.

Natal Venus in Virgo

You always try to look neat and tidy, and are horribly self-conscious whenever you don't meet your own high standards. There's a Virgoan modesty to most of your clothes, and you have a preference for small prints and plain colours. Anything too gaudy, cheap or flashy really isn't your style.

Natal Venus in Libra

Elegant, stylish and understated, you have classic good taste. You have a deep-seated need to present yourself at your best and may spend a lot of money on buying the perfect clothes and shoes. It's also important for you to smell nice, so you love soaps and scents.

Natal Venus in Scorpio

You exude mystery, charisma and the impression that still waters most definitely run deep. It's important for you to make a style statement, but that's more about doing your own thing than following the latest fashions. You love wearing strong colours and you also have a nice line in sunglasses.

Natal Venus in Sagittarius

Laid back and relaxed, that's you. You're happiest in casual clothes, such as jeans and T-shirts, that don't hamper your movements and can easily be replaced whenever your accident-prone tendencies get the better of you. Clothes from other cultures or countries can appeal to you, too.

Natal Venus in Capricorn

You dress to impress, in formal clothes or sophisticated outfits that suit you and exude first-class quality and quiet good taste. Anything brash or flash is beneath your very considerable dignity, and you avoid high fashion, too, because you prefer to create your own timeless style.

Natal Venus in Aquarius

Of all the Venus signs, this is the most charismatic. Add glamour, style and poise, and you're a head-turning proposition. You're happiest when wearing clothes that reflect your individuality, rather than because they're what's expected of you for some reason. Show off your great ankles!

Natal Venus in Pisces

There's something ethereal and delicate about you, regardless of your sex. Maybe you choose clothes that are airy and pretty, or colours that are subtle and pastel. Anything harsh is unlikely to suit you because that isn't your style at all. Beautiful shoes and boots may be a weakness of yours.

✳✳ What makes
✳✳ you get up
✳✳ every day?

Mars is a planet that loves to feel enthusiastic. In fact, it's vital for Mars to have an interest in life. What does your natal Mars tell you about your own enthusiasms and your reasons for bouncing out of bed each morning?

Natal Mars in Aries

Life always holds the promise of fresh excitements and new experiences, so you want to get the very best out of each day. It's a huge thrill whenever you launch a new project or enterprise, especially if it will throw up a few challenges or risks. You hate playing safe!

Natal Mars in Taurus

You want each day to be productive, especially if that means creating something yourself. You need to feel grounded, so being out in nature is especially enjoyable and satisfying for you. Gardening and country walks are good, but so are making money and acquiring possessions.

Natal Mars in Gemini

You're most excited when you're never sure what the day will bring, so you try not to have every minute accounted for in advance. That's such a boring prospect! You can't resist buying gadgets because you love having something new to play with.

Natal Mars in Cancer

Whatever you do in life, it must offer you emotional satisfaction. Maybe you can't explain what that is but you certainly know it when you've got it. Building up a collection of treasured objects, especially if they have family or historic connections, makes you feel good.

Natal Mars in Leo

Put some creative or artistic expression into each day! You're happiest when you have an exciting and stimulating project on the go, because you find it inspirational and satisfying. It also helps to have an appreciative audience so you know your efforts aren't being ignored.

Natal Mars in Virgo

Your natural curiosity always keeps you active and amused. Questions such as 'why' and 'how' scamper through your mind, seeking answers. It's also essential for you to express your practical and methodical talents, whether at work or simply as you go through each day.

Natal Mars in Libra

Connecting with other people is a big motivation for you. You like to feel that you're part of a team, whether for work or personal reasons. Playing fair and seeing that justice is done are also vitally important, making you eager to support good causes and defend anyone in trouble.

Natal Mars in Scorpio

You must have a purpose in life and something that gives you emotional satisfaction. Ideally, it also offers you spiritual nourishment and meaning, whether it's a relationship, a hobby or a belief, and can help you to process what can sometimes be very turbulent emotions.

Natal Mars in Sagittarius

Almost anything will make you spring out of bed, provided it awakens your ever-present enthusiasm and inexhaustible optimism. You love discovering new hobbies that set light to your imagination, especially if they involve travel or learning something new.

Natal Mars in Capricorn

Ambition and purpose are your watchwords, spurring you into action and making you determined to get the very best out of each day. However, you must beware of working yourself into the ground or behaving ruthlessly when dealing with competitors.

Natal Mars in Aquarius

You have such a strong desire to make the world a better place, whether in big or little ways, that you can get very heated when encouraging others to see things your way. You'll fire off emails, be a keyboard warrior on social media or support a charity. But you must do something!

Natal Mars in Pisces

Finding a purpose in life is essential for you, otherwise you can feel adrift in a sea of uncertainty and problems. Helping others can be a great way to help yourself, too, whether you do it voluntarily or for a living, because you want to alleviate suffering whenever you see it.

Keeping the peace

Venus is a planet of harmony and the sign she occupies at any given time determines whether that harmony comes easily. Look up Venus's current sign in the back of the book or online to see how you can keep life on an even keel at the moment.

When Venus is in Aries

It's not easy to keep everyone happy. Those around you want to have everything their own way or they might show every sign of enjoying an argument now and then. This is a good time to sort out your differences, preferably politely but firmly. Burn off residual anger through physical exercise, whether outdoors or in the bedroom.

When Venus is in Taurus

Be wary of anyone who wants to use money as a means of taking control or showing who's boss. A delicious meal, whether eaten at home or in a restaurant, could soothe wounded feelings. If you're looking for a break, get out into a garden or visit your favourite beauty spot.

When Venus is in Gemini

Don't dismiss the benefits of discussions, negotiations and saying the right thing at the right time. You must also be prepared to listen as well as talk! Be amenable and prepared to meet others halfway, and make the most of your innate charm. A light touch is invaluable at the moment.

When Venus is in Cancer

Take care not to become defensive or to retreat into a moody huff over the slightest disagreement, otherwise nothing will be resolved. Domestic difficulties have the power to unsettle you so do your best to face up to them and find a solution that suits everyone.

When Venus is in Leo

Problems connected with the family, children or artistic activities are possible, but are they being over-dramatized? Try not to get drawn into anyone's ego trips or demands, especially if they pull rank on you. You should also be aware of your own tendencies to hog the limelight right now.

When Venus is in Virgo

You may have to sort out difficulties connected with work or health. The best way to do this is to focus on the facts and to analyse what's going on, but beware of being too eager to play the blame game. Take care, too, not to be too critical of others.

When Venus is in Libra

Dealing with other people could be tricky, especially if you fail to see eye to eye with them. The best way round this is to muster all your powers of charm and tact, and to reach compromises whenever possible. It's important to find balance and harmony at the moment.

When Venus is in Scorpio

Close relationships need careful handling, especially if you're dealing with someone's stubbornness, controlling behaviour or jealousy. Be aware that you might show some of these tendencies, too! Someone could freeze you out or be icily polite, while refusing to say what's upset them.

When Venus is in Sagittarius

Choose your words carefully, otherwise you might say the wrong thing or accidentally make a compliment sound more like an insult. Appealing to someone's sense of humour may turn out to be a very wise move. It can also help to adopt a philosophical approach.

When Venus is in Capricorn

There could be rifts or disagreements connected with work, social status or bureaucracy, or about someone's workaholic tendencies. Try to appeal to other people's common sense and dignity, and set a good example yourself. Avoid clamping down on your emotions for self-protective reasons.

When Venus is in Aquarius

Controversial topics need to be tackled with diplomacy, but you may find that everyone is too obstinate to want to find much common ground. Also, someone may enjoy being as shocking or disruptive as they possibly can, but do you really have to rise to the bait in the way they expect?

When Venus is in Pisces

If trouble brews, you'll find it hard to know what's going on because so much is confusing or even deliberately misleading. Handle people carefully and keep an eye out for anyone who wants to be regarded as a saint or victim – including yourself!

Putting your foot down

There are times in even the most easy-going relationship when things go slightly wrong. As a result, tempers flare. Or do they? Not everyone finds it easy to lose their rag, even if they are fuming inside. Here's the lowdown on how each Mars sign reacts when annoyed – not only you, but all the other people in your life.

Natal Mars in Aries

Whenever you lose your temper, your anger bursts into sudden life, rages for a few frenzied minutes and then dies down as quickly as it began. Almost anything can make you see red, but the most common triggers include being kept waiting, having to follow someone else's lead and being ignored.

Natal Mars in Taurus

It takes a lot to get you riled, but when you do everyone knows about it. Among the things that really make you angry are problems connected with possessions, personal finances and when you don't get what you want, because compromise doesn't always come easily to you.

Natal Mars in Gemini

Words are your weapon and you use them well, especially when you're fuming. You can be sarcastic, cutting and withering. Irritations that really get to you include other people's ignorance and stupidity, problems with transport and infuriating delays when you're in a tearing hurry.

Natal Mars in Cancer

You might feel your fury building but it can then either become inaccessible or morph into being sulky or moody about something completely different. All sorts of things make you seethe inside, from cruelty to children to feeling that someone is having a go at you.

Natal Mars in Leo

Do you believe that losing your temper is beneath you? Dignity and pride often stop you getting angry, but when you really do blow your top it can be dramatic and theatrical. You can't stand being bossed about, being treated disrespectfully or feeling thwarted.

Natal Mars in Virgo

Inefficiency, laziness, slovenly habits and cutting corners are all guaranteed to infuriate you and sharpen your tongue. You don't mince words, so anyone who fails to meet your own high standards is left in no doubt about what they've done wrong.

Natal Mars in Libra

You like to give others the benefit of the doubt whenever possible and do your best to remain courteous and civil if you do lose your temper. Your powerful sense of fair play means that you object strongly whenever you hear about injustices or prejudices.

Natal Mars in Scorpio

Your anger simmers until it finally comes to the boil, at which point it erupts into sarcastic and even vitriolic fury. You know how to bear a grudge and keep a score, long after the argument is over. Triggers include lack of loyalty, jealousy and being lied to.

Natal Mars in Sagittarius

If you're angry with someone, you most certainly let them know it. You can be rude and brutally honest, especially if you get carried away in the heat of the moment. Dishonesty and lack of moral courage are particular flashpoints for you.

Natal Mars in Capricorn

The tighter your emotional control, the harder it is to get angry, yet you can still be seething inside. Whenever you do allow yourself to let rip, you know how to wound with words. You can't bear being embarrassed or criticized for working hard.

Natal Mars in Aquarius

There's an icy detachment to your anger, helping you to keep cool mentally so you can argue your case with precision. You detest it if you're expected to obey petty or ludicrous rules, and you're prepared to fight for major causes if necessary.

Natal Mars in Pisces

Losing your temper isn't easy. It's there one minute and gone the next, and to make matters worse you can feel guilty in advance about hurting someone's feelings. One thing you absolutely won't tolerate is knowing that others are suffering or being abused.

Venus tables

Look up the year you were born and then zero in to find your Venus sign. Full instructions on how to do this are given on pages 30–32.

DATE	TIME	SIGN	MOTION	DATE	TIME	SIGN	MOTION
6 Jan 1955	06:48	SAG		6 Dec 1957	15:25	AQU	
6 Feb 1955	01:15	CAP		8 Jan 1958	02:47	AQU	R
4 Mar 1955	20:21	AQU		18 Feb 1958	06:17	AQU	D
30 Mar 1955	11:30	PIS		6 Apr 1958	15:59	PIS	
24 Apr 1955	15:12	ARI		5 May 1958	11:58	ARI	
19 May 1955	13:35	TAU		1 Jun 1958	04:07	TAU	
13 Jun 1955	08:37	GEM		26 Jun 1958	23:08	GEM	
8 Jul 1955	00:15	CAN		22 Jul 1958	05:25	CAN	
1 Aug 1955	11:42	LEO		16 Aug 1958	01:28	LEO	
25 Aug 1955	18:52	VIR		9 Sep 1958	12:35	VIR	
18 Sep 1955	22:40	LIB		3 Oct 1958	16:43	LIB	
13 Oct 1955	00:38	SCO		27 Oct 1958	16:26	SCO	
6 Nov 1955	02:02	SAG		20 Nov 1958	13:59	SAG	
30 Nov 1955	03:42	CAP		14 Dec 1958	10:54	CAP	
24 Dec 1955	06:52	AQU		7 Jan 1959	08:16	AQU	
17 Jan 1956	14:21	PIS		31 Jan 1959	07:28	PIS	
11 Feb 1956	07:46	ARI		24 Feb 1959	10:52	ARI	
7 Mar 1956	21:31	TAU		20 Mar 1959	21:55	TAU	
4 Apr 1956	07:22	GEM		14 Apr 1959	21:07	GEM	
8 May 1956	02:16	CAN		10 May 1959	15:44	CAN	
31 May 1956	18:04	CAN	R	6 Jun 1959	22:42	LEO	
23 Jun 1956	12:10	GEM	R	8 Jul 1959	12:07	VIR	
13 Jul 1956	21:20	GEM	D	10 Aug 1959	23:16	VIR	R
4 Aug 1956	09:48	CAN		20 Sep 1959	03:01	LEO	R
8 Sep 1956	09:23	LEO		22 Sep 1959	17:15	LEO	D
6 Oct 1956	03:12	VIR		25 Sep 1959	08:14	VIR	
31 Oct 1956	19:39	LIB		9 Nov 1959	18:10	LIB	
25 Nov 1956	13:01	SCO		7 Dec 1959	16:41	SCO	
19 Dec 1956	19:06	SAG		2 Jan 1960	08:42	SAG	
12 Jan 1957	20:22	CAP		27 Jan 1960	04:45	CAP	
5 Feb 1957	20:16	AQU		20 Feb 1960	16:47	AQU	
1 Mar 1957	20:39	PIS		16 Mar 1960	01:53	PIS	
25 Mar 1957	22:45	ARI		9 Apr 1960	10:32	ARI	
19 Apr 1957	03:28	TAU		3 May 1960	19:55	TAU	
13 May 1957	11:07	GEM		28 May 1960	06:10	GEM	
6 Jun 1957	21:34	CAN		21 Jun 1960	16:33	CAN	
1 Jul 1957	10:42	LEO		16 Jul 1960	02:11	LEO	
26 Jul 1957	03:09	VIR		9 Aug 1960	10:53	VIR	
20 Aug 1957	00:43	LIB		2 Sep 1960	19:29	LIB	
14 Sep 1957	06:19	SCO		27 Sep 1960	05:12	SCO	
10 Oct 1957	01:15	SAG		21 Oct 1960	17:11	SAG	
5 Nov 1957	23:45	CAP		15 Nov 1960	08:57	CAP	

DATE	TIME	SIGN	MOTION	DATE	TIME	SIGN	MOTION
10 Dec 1960	08:34	AQU		8 Sep 1964	04:53	LEO	
5 Jan 1961	03:30	PIS		5 Oct 1964	18:10	VIR	
2 Feb 1961	04:45	ARI		31 Oct 1964	08:54	LIB	
20 Mar 1961	20:13	ARI	R	25 Nov 1964	01:24	SCO	
2 May 1961	04:15	ARI	D	19 Dec 1964	07:02	SAG	
5 Jun 1961	19:24	TAU		12 Jan 1965	08:00	CAP	
7 Jul 1961	04:32	GEM		5 Feb 1965	07:41	AQU	
3 Aug 1961	15:28	CAN		1 Mar 1965	07:55	PIS	
29 Aug 1961	14:18	LEO		25 Mar 1965	09:53	ARI	
23 Sep 1961	15:42	VIR		18 Apr 1965	14:30	TAU	
18 Oct 1961	02:58	LIB		12 May 1965	22:07	GEM	
11 Nov 1961	05:32	SCO		6 Jun 1965	08:38	CAN	
5 Dec 1961	03:39	SAG		30 Jun 1965	21:59	LEO	
29 Dec 1961	00:06	CAP		25 Jul 1965	14:51	VIR	
21 Jan 1962	20:30	AQU		19 Aug 1965	13:06	LIB	
14 Feb 1962	18:08	PIS		13 Sep 1965	19:50	SCO	
10 Mar 1962	18:28	ARI		9 Oct 1965	16:45	SAG	
3 Apr 1962	23:04	TAU		5 Nov 1965	19:35	CAP	
28 Apr 1962	09:22	GEM		7 Dec 1965	04:36	AQU	
23 May 1962	02:46	CAN		5 Jan 1966	16:21	AQU	R
17 Jun 1962	05:30	LEO		6 Feb 1966	12:46	CAP	R
12 Jul 1962	22:31	VIR		15 Feb 1966	18:41	CAP	D
8 Aug 1962	17:13	LIB		25 Feb 1966	10:54	AQU	
7 Sep 1962	00:10	SCO		6 Apr 1966	15:53	PIS	
23 Oct 1962	04:14	SCO	R	5 May 1966	04:33	ARI	
3 Dec 1962	11:26	SCO	D	31 May 1966	18:00	TAU	
6 Jan 1963	17:35	SAG		26 Jun 1966	11:40	GEM	
5 Feb 1963	20:35	CAP		21 Jul 1966	17:11	CAN	
4 Mar 1963	11:41	AQU		15 Aug 1966	12:47	LEO	
30 Mar 1963	00:59	PIS		8 Sep 1966	23:40	VIR	
24 Apr 1963	03:39	ARI		3 Oct 1966	03:44	LIB	
19 May 1963	01:20	TAU		27 Oct 1966	03:27	SCO	
12 Jun 1963	19:56	GEM		20 Nov 1966	01:06	SAG	
7 Jul 1963	11:17	CAN		13 Dec 1966	22:08	CAP	
31 Jul 1963	22:28	LEO		6 Jan 1967	19:35	AQU	
25 Aug 1963	05:48	VIR		30 Jan 1967	18:53	PIS	
18 Sep 1963	09:42	LIB		23 Feb 1967	22:29	ARI	
12 Oct 1963	11:49	SCO		20 Mar 1967	09:55	TAU	
5 Nov 1963	13:25	SAG		14 Apr 1967	09:54	GEM	
29 Nov 1963	15:21	CAP		10 May 1967	06:04	CAN	
23 Dec 1963	18:53	AQU		6 Jun 1967	16:47	LEO	
17 Jan 1964	02:53	PIS		8 Jul 1967	22:11	VIR	
10 Feb 1964	21:09	ARI		8 Aug 1967	14:29	VIR	R
7 Mar 1964	12:38	TAU		9 Sep 1967	11:57	LEO	R
4 Apr 1964	03:02	GEM		20 Sep 1967	09:34	LEO	D
9 May 1964	03:15	CAN		1 Oct 1967	18:06	VIR	
29 May 1964	10:29	CAN	R	9 Nov 1967	16:32	LIB	
17 Jun 1964	18:17	GEM	R	7 Dec 1967	08:47	SCO	
11 Jul 1964	13:00	GEM	D	1 Jan 1968	22:37	SAG	
5 Aug 1964	08:52	CAN		26 Jan 1968	17:34	CAP	

DATE	TIME	SIGN	MOTION	DATE	TIME	SIGN	MOTION
20 Feb 1968	04:55	AQU		5 Nov 1971	00:30	SAG	
15 Mar 1968	13:31	PIS		29 Nov 1971	02:41	CAP	
8 Apr 1968	21:48	ARI		23 Dec 1971	06:32	AQU	
3 May 1968	06:56	TAU		16 Jan 1972	15:01	PIS	
27 May 1968	17:02	GEM		10 Feb 1972	10:08	ARI	
21 Jun 1968	03:20	CAN		7 Mar 1972	03:25	TAU	
15 Jul 1968	12:58	LEO		3 Apr 1972	22:47	GEM	
8 Aug 1968	21:48	VIR		10 May 1972	13:51	CAN	
2 Sep 1968	06:39	LIB		27 May 1972	03:14	CAN	R
26 Sep 1968	16:45	SCO		11 Jun 1972	20:08	GEM	R
21 Oct 1968	05:16	SAG		9 Jul 1972	04:55	GEM	D
14 Nov 1968	21:47	CAP		6 Aug 1972	01:26	CAN	
9 Dec 1968	22:39	AQU		7 Sep 1972	23:26	LEO	
4 Jan 1969	20:06	PIS		5 Oct 1972	08:33	VIR	
2 Feb 1969	04:44	ARI		30 Oct 1972	21:39	LIB	
18 Mar 1969	11:49	ARI	R	24 Nov 1972	13:23	SCO	
29 Apr 1969	19:20	ARI	D	18 Dec 1972	18:33	SAG	
6 Jun 1969	01:48	TAU		11 Jan 1973	19:14	CAP	
6 Jul 1969	22:03	GEM		4 Feb 1973	18:42	AQU	
3 Aug 1969	05:29	CAN		28 Feb 1973	18:44	PIS	
29 Aug 1969	02:47	LEO		24 Mar 1973	20:34	ARI	
23 Sep 1969	03:25	VIR		18 Apr 1973	01:05	TAU	
17 Oct 1969	14:17	LIB		12 May 1973	08:42	GEM	
10 Nov 1969	16:39	SCO		5 Jun 1973	19:19	CAN	
4 Dec 1969	14:40	SAG		30 Jun 1973	08:55	LEO	
28 Dec 1969	11:03	CAP		25 Jul 1973	02:12	VIR	
21 Jan 1970	07:25	AQU		19 Aug 1973	01:10	LIB	
14 Feb 1970	05:03	PIS		13 Sep 1973	09:04	SCO	
10 Mar 1970	05:24	ARI		9 Oct 1973	08:07	SAG	
3 Apr 1970	10:04	TAU		5 Nov 1973	15:39	CAP	
27 Apr 1970	20:33	GEM		7 Dec 1973	21:37	AQU	
22 May 1970	14:19	CAN		3 Jan 1974	06:07	AQU	R
16 Jun 1970	17:48	LEO		29 Jan 1974	19:50	CAP	R
12 Jul 1970	12:16	VIR		13 Feb 1974	07:28	CAP	D
8 Aug 1970	09:59	LIB		28 Feb 1974	14:24	AQU	
7 Sep 1970	01:53	SCO		6 Apr 1974	14:16	PIS	
20 Oct 1970	15:57	SCO	R	4 May 1974	20:21	ARI	
1 Dec 1970	00:03	SCO	D	31 May 1974	07:18	TAU	
7 Jan 1971	00:59	SAG		25 Jun 1974	23:43	GEM	
5 Feb 1971	14:56	CAP		21 Jul 1974	04:33	CAN	
4 Mar 1971	02:24	AQU		14 Aug 1974	23:46	LEO	
29 Mar 1971	14:01	PIS		8 Sep 1974	10:27	VIR	
23 Apr 1971	15:43	ARI		2 Oct 1974	14:26	LIB	
18 May 1971	12:47	TAU		26 Oct 1974	14:12	SCO	
12 Jun 1971	06:57	GEM		19 Nov 1974	11:56	SAG	
6 Jul 1971	22:02	CAN		13 Dec 1974	09:05	CAP	
31 Jul 1971	09:14	LEO		6 Jan 1975	06:39	AQU	
24 Aug 1971	16:25	VIR		30 Jan 1975	06:04	PIS	
17 Sep 1971	20:25	LIB		23 Feb 1975	09:52	ARI	
11 Oct 1971	22:42	SCO		19 Mar 1975	21:42	TAU	

DATE	TIME	SIGN	MOTION	DATE	TIME	SIGN	MOTION
13 Apr 1975	22:25	GEM		7 Jan 1979	06:37	SAG	
9 May 1975	20:11	CAN		5 Feb 1979	09:15	CAP	
6 Jun 1975	10:54	LEO		3 Mar 1979	17:18	AQU	
9 Jul 1975	11:06	VIR		29 Mar 1979	03:17	PIS	
6 Aug 1975	05:21	VIR	R	23 Apr 1979	04:02	ARI	
2 Sep 1975	15:34	LEO	R	18 May 1979	00:28	TAU	
18 Sep 1975	01:46	LEO	D	11 Jun 1979	18:13	GEM	
4 Oct 1975	05:19	VIR		6 Jul 1979	09:02	CAN	
9 Nov 1975	13:51	LIB		30 Jul 1979	20:06	LEO	
7 Dec 1975	00:28	SCO		24 Aug 1979	03:16	VIR	
1 Jan 1976	12:14	SAG		17 Sep 1979	07:21	LIB	
26 Jan 1976	06:08	CAP		11 Oct 1979	09:47	SCO	
19 Feb 1976	16:50	AQU		4 Nov 1979	11:49	SAG	
15 Mar 1976	00:59	PIS		28 Nov 1979	14:19	CAP	
8 Apr 1976	08:55	ARI		22 Dec 1979	18:34	AQU	
2 May 1976	17:48	TAU		16 Jan 1980	03:36	PIS	
27 May 1976	03:43	GEM		9 Feb 1980	23:39	ARI	
20 Jun 1976	13:55	CAN		6 Mar 1980	18:54	TAU	
14 Jul 1976	23:35	LEO		3 Apr 1980	19:46	GEM	
8 Aug 1976	08:35	VIR		12 May 1980	20:52	CAN	
1 Sep 1976	17:44	LIB		24 May 1980	20:10	CAN	R
26 Sep 1976	04:16	SCO		5 Jun 1980	05:44	GEM	R
20 Oct 1976	17:22	SAG		6 Jul 1980	21:15	GEM	D
14 Nov 1976	10:41	CAP		6 Aug 1980	14:24	CAN	
9 Dec 1976	12:52	AQU		7 Sep 1980	17:57	LEO	
4 Jan 1977	13:01	PIS		4 Oct 1980	23:06	VIR	
2 Feb 1977	05:54	ARI		30 Oct 1980	10:37	LIB	
16 Mar 1977	03:01	ARI	R	24 Nov 1980	01:34	SCO	
27 Apr 1977	09:49	ARI	D	18 Dec 1980	06:20	SAG	
6 Jun 1977	06:10	TAU		11 Jan 1981	06:48	CAP	
6 Jul 1977	15:08	GEM		4 Feb 1981	06:07	AQU	
2 Aug 1977	19:18	CAN		28 Feb 1981	06:01	PIS	
28 Aug 1977	15:09	LEO		24 Mar 1981	07:42	ARI	
22 Sep 1977	15:05	VIR		17 Apr 1981	12:07	TAU	
17 Oct 1977	01:37	LIB		11 May 1981	19:44	GEM	
10 Nov 1977	03:51	SCO		5 Jun 1981	06:29	CAN	
4 Dec 1977	01:48	SAG		29 Jun 1981	20:19	LEO	
27 Dec 1977	22:09	CAP		24 Jul 1981	14:03	VIR	
20 Jan 1978	18:29	AQU		18 Aug 1981	13:44	LIB	
13 Feb 1978	16:06	PIS		12 Sep 1981	22:50	SCO	
9 Mar 1978	16:28	ARI		9 Oct 1981	00:04	SAG	
2 Apr 1978	21:13	TAU		5 Nov 1981	12:39	CAP	
27 Apr 1978	07:53	GEM		8 Dec 1981	20:52	AQU	
22 May 1978	02:03	CAN		31 Dec 1981	19:45	AQU	R
16 Jun 1978	06:18	LEO		23 Jan 1982	02:56	CAP	R
12 Jul 1978	02:13	VIR		10 Feb 1982	20:38	CAP	D
8 Aug 1978	03:08	LIB		2 Mar 1982	11:25	AQU	
7 Sep 1978	05:07	SCO		6 Apr 1982	12:20	PIS	
18 Oct 1978	03:58	SCO	R	4 May 1982	12:26	ARI	
28 Nov 1978	13:10	SCO	D	30 May 1982	21:01	TAU	

DATE	TIME	SIGN	MOTION	DATE	TIME	SIGN	MOTION
25 Jun 1982	12:12	GEM		20 Jan 1986	05:35	AQU	
20 Jul 1982	16:20	CAN		13 Feb 1986	03:10	PIS	
14 Aug 1982	11:09	LEO		9 Mar 1986	03:31	ARI	
7 Sep 1982	21:37	VIR		2 Apr 1986	08:18	TAU	
2 Oct 1982	01:32	LIB		26 Apr 1986	19:09	GEM	
26 Oct 1982	01:18	SCO		21 May 1986	13:45	CAN	
18 Nov 1982	23:06	SAG		15 Jun 1986	18:51	LEO	
12 Dec 1982	20:19	CAP		11 Jul 1986	16:22	VIR	
5 Jan 1983	17:58	AQU		7 Aug 1986	20:45	LIB	
29 Jan 1983	17:31	PIS		7 Sep 1986	10:15	SCO	
22 Feb 1983	21:34	ARI		15 Oct 1986	16:33	SCO	R
19 Mar 1983	09:51	TAU		26 Nov 1986	02:47	SCO	D
13 Apr 1983	11:25	GEM		7 Jan 1987	10:19	SAG	
9 May 1983	10:56	CAN		5 Feb 1987	03:03	CAP	
6 Jun 1983	06:03	LEO		3 Mar 1987	07:55	AQU	
10 Jul 1983	05:24	VIR		28 Mar 1987	16:19	PIS	
3 Aug 1983	19:44	VIR	R	22 Apr 1987	16:07	ARI	
27 Aug 1983	11:43	LEO	R	17 May 1987	11:55	TAU	
15 Sep 1983	17:22	LEO	D	11 Jun 1987	05:15	GEM	
5 Oct 1983	19:34	VIR		5 Jul 1987	19:49	CAN	
9 Nov 1983	10:52	LIB		30 Jul 1987	06:49	LEO	
6 Dec 1983	16:14	SCO		23 Aug 1987	14:00	VIR	
1 Jan 1984	01:59	SAG		16 Sep 1987	18:11	LIB	
25 Jan 1984	18:50	CAP		10 Oct 1987	20:48	SCO	
19 Feb 1984	04:52	AQU		3 Nov 1987	23:03	SAG	
14 Mar 1984	12:34	PIS		28 Nov 1987	01:51	CAP	
7 Apr 1984	20:13	ARI		22 Dec 1987	06:28	AQU	
2 May 1984	04:53	TAU		15 Jan 1988	16:03	PIS	
26 May 1984	14:39	GEM		9 Feb 1988	13:03	ARI	
20 Jun 1984	00:48	CAN		6 Mar 1988	10:20	TAU	
14 Jul 1984	10:30	LEO		3 Apr 1988	17:07	GEM	
7 Aug 1984	19:39	VIR		17 May 1988	16:26	CAN	
1 Sep 1984	05:06	LIB		22 May 1988	13:26	CAN	R
25 Sep 1984	16:04	SCO		27 May 1988	07:35	GEM	R
20 Oct 1984	05:45	SAG		4 Jul 1988	14:09	GEM	D
13 Nov 1984	23:54	CAP		6 Aug 1988	23:23	CAN	
9 Dec 1984	03:26	AQU		7 Sep 1988	11:37	LEO	
4 Jan 1985	06:23	PIS		4 Oct 1988	13:14	VIR	
2 Feb 1985	08:28	ARI		29 Oct 1988	23:19	LIB	
13 Mar 1985	18:17	ARI	R	23 Nov 1988	13:33	SCO	
25 Apr 1985	00:09	ARI	D	17 Dec 1988	17:55	SAG	
6 Jun 1985	08:52	TAU		10 Jan 1989	18:07	CAP	
6 Jul 1985	08:01	GEM		3 Feb 1989	17:14	AQU	
2 Aug 1985	09:09	CAN		27 Feb 1989	16:58	PIS	
28 Aug 1985	03:38	LEO		23 Mar 1989	18:31	ARI	
22 Sep 1985	02:52	VIR		16 Apr 1989	22:52	TAU	
16 Oct 1985	13:03	LIB		11 May 1989	06:28	GEM	
9 Nov 1985	15:07	SCO		4 Jun 1989	17:17	CAN	
3 Dec 1985	12:59	SAG		29 Jun 1989	07:21	LEO	
27 Dec 1985	09:17	CAP		24 Jul 1989	01:31	VIR	

DATE	TIME	SIGN	MOTION	DATE	TIME	SIGN	MOTION
18 Aug 1989	01:57	LIB		2 Feb 1993	12:37	ARI	
12 Sep 1989	12:22	SCO		11 Mar 1993	09:28	ARI	R
8 Oct 1989	15:59	SAG		22 Apr 1993	14:13	ARI	D
5 Nov 1989	10:12	CAP		6 Jun 1993	10:02	TAU	
10 Dec 1989	04:53	AQU		6 Jul 1993	00:21	GEM	
29 Dec 1989	08:50	AQU	R	1 Aug 1993	22:38	CAN	
16 Jan 1990	15:22	CAP	R	27 Aug 1993	15:48	LEO	
8 Feb 1990	09:16	CAP	D	21 Sep 1993	14:22	VIR	
3 Mar 1990	17:51	AQU		16 Oct 1993	00:12	LIB	
6 Apr 1990	09:13	PIS		9 Nov 1993	02:06	SCO	
4 May 1990	03:52	ARI		2 Dec 1993	23:53	SAG	
30 May 1990	10:13	TAU		26 Dec 1993	20:09	CAP	
25 Jun 1990	00:14	GEM		19 Jan 1994	16:27	AQU	
20 Jul 1990	03:40	CAN		12 Feb 1994	14:04	PIS	
13 Aug 1990	22:04	LEO		8 Mar 1994	14:27	ARI	
7 Sep 1990	08:20	VIR		1 Apr 1994	19:20	TAU	
1 Oct 1990	12:12	LIB		26 Apr 1994	06:23	GEM	
25 Oct 1990	12:03	SCO		21 May 1994	01:26	CAN	
18 Nov 1990	09:58	SAG		15 Jun 1994	07:23	LEO	
12 Dec 1990	07:18	CAP		11 Jul 1994	06:32	VIR	
5 Jan 1991	05:03	AQU		7 Aug 1994	14:36	LIB	
29 Jan 1991	04:44	PIS		7 Sep 1994	17:12	SCO	
22 Feb 1991	09:01	ARI		13 Oct 1994	05:41	SCO	R
18 Mar 1991	21:44	TAU		23 Nov 1994	16:57	SCO	D
13 Apr 1991	00:10	GEM		7 Jan 1995	12:06	SAG	
9 May 1991	01:28	CAN		4 Feb 1995	20:11	CAP	
6 Jun 1991	01:16	LEO		2 Mar 1995	22:10	AQU	
11 Jul 1991	05:06	VIR		28 Mar 1995	05:10	PIS	
1 Aug 1991	10:35	VIR	R	22 Apr 1995	04:06	ARI	
21 Aug 1991	15:05	LEO	R	16 May 1995	23:21	TAU	
13 Sep 1991	08:56	LEO	D	10 Jun 1995	16:18	GEM	
6 Oct 1991	21:15	VIR		5 Jul 1995	06:38	CAN	
9 Nov 1991	06:36	LIB		29 Jul 1995	17:31	LEO	
6 Dec 1991	07:20	SCO		23 Aug 1995	00:42	VIR	
31 Dec 1991	15:19	SAG		16 Sep 1995	05:00	LIB	
25 Jan 1992	07:14	CAP		10 Oct 1995	07:48	SCO	
18 Feb 1992	16:40	AQU		3 Nov 1995	10:18	SAG	
13 Mar 1992	23:56	PIS		27 Nov 1995	13:23	CAP	
7 Apr 1992	07:15	ARI		21 Dec 1995	18:22	AQU	
1 May 1992	15:41	TAU		15 Jan 1996	04:30	PIS	
26 May 1992	01:17	GEM		9 Feb 1996	02:30	ARI	
19 Jun 1992	11:22	CAN		6 Mar 1996	02:00	TAU	
13 Jul 1992	21:06	LEO		3 Apr 1996	15:25	GEM	
7 Aug 1992	06:25	VIR		20 May 1996	06:08	GEM	R
31 Aug 1992	16:08	LIB		2 Jul 1996	06:51	GEM	D
25 Sep 1992	03:31	SCO		7 Aug 1996	06:14	CAN	
19 Oct 1992	17:46	SAG		7 Sep 1996	05:07	LEO	
13 Nov 1992	12:47	CAP		4 Oct 1996	03:21	VIR	
8 Dec 1992	17:49	AQU		29 Oct 1996	12:01	LIB	
3 Jan 1993	23:53	PIS		23 Nov 1996	01:34	SCO	

DATE	TIME	SIGN	MOTION	DATE	TIME	SIGN	MOTION
17 Dec 1996	05:33	SAG		25 May 2000	12:14	GEM	
10 Jan 1997	05:31	CAP		18 Jun 2000	22:14	CAN	
3 Feb 1997	04:27	AQU		13 Jul 2000	08:02	LEO	
27 Feb 1997	04:00	PIS		6 Aug 2000	17:32	VIR	
23 Mar 1997	05:20	ARI		24 Sep 2000	15:25	SCO	
16 Apr 1997	09:42	TAU		19 Oct 2000	06:18	SAG	
10 May 1997	17:20	GEM		13 Nov 2000	02:14	CAP	
4 Jun 1997	04:17	CAN		8 Dec 2000	08:48	AQU	
28 Jun 1997	18:37	LEO		3 Jan 2001	18:13	PIS	
23 Jul 1997	13:16	VIR		2 Feb 2001	19:13	ARI	
17 Aug 1997	14:30	LIB		9 Mar 2001	01:07	ARI	R
12 Sep 1997	02:16	SCO		20 Apr 2001	04:34	ARI	D
8 Oct 1997	08:25	SAG		6 Jun 2001	10:24	TAU	
5 Nov 1997	08:50	CAP		5 Jul 2001	16:43	GEM	
12 Dec 1997	04:38	AQU		1 Aug 2001	12:17	CAN	
26 Dec 1997	21:21	AQU	R	27 Aug 2001	04:12	LEO	
9 Jan 1998	21:03	CAP	R	21 Sep 2001	02:09	VIR	
5 Feb 1998	21:26	CAP	D	15 Oct 2001	11:42	LIB	
4 Mar 1998	16:14	AQU		8 Nov 2001	13:28	SCO	
6 Apr 1998	05:38	PIS		2 Dec 2001	11:11	SAG	
3 May 1998	19:16	ARI		26 Dec 2001	07:25	CAP	
29 May 1998	23:32	TAU		19 Jan 2002	03:42	AQU	
24 Jun 1998	12:27	GEM		12 Feb 2002	01:17	PIS	
19 Jul 1998	15:16	CAN		8 Mar 2002	01:41	ARI	
13 Aug 1998	09:19	LEO		1 Apr 2002	06:39	TAU	
6 Sep 1998	19:24	VIR		25 Apr 2002	17:56	GEM	
30 Sep 1998	23:13	LIB		20 May 2002	13:27	CAN	
24 Oct 1998	23:06	SCO		14 Jun 2002	20:16	LEO	
17 Nov 1998	21:06	SAG		10 Jul 2002	21:08	VIR	
11 Dec 1998	18:32	CAP		7 Aug 2002	09:08	LIB	
4 Jan 1999	16:25	AQU		8 Sep 2002	03:04	SCO	
28 Jan 1999	16:16	PIS		10 Oct 2002	18:35	SCO	R
21 Feb 1999	20:49	ARI		21 Nov 2002	07:13	SCO	D
18 Mar 1999	09:59	TAU		7 Jan 2003	13:07	SAG	
12 Apr 1999	13:16	GEM		4 Feb 2003	13:26	CAP	
8 May 1999	16:28	CAN		2 Mar 2003	12:39	AQU	
5 Jun 1999	21:24	LEO		27 Mar 2003	18:13	PIS	
12 Jul 1999	15:17	VIR		21 Apr 2003	16:17	ARI	
30 Jul 1999	01:42	VIR	R	16 May 2003	10:58	TAU	
15 Aug 1999	14:11	LEO	R	10 Jun 2003	03:31	GEM	
11 Sep 1999	00:23	LEO	D	4 Jul 2003	17:38	CAN	
7 Oct 1999	16:50	VIR		29 Jul 2003	04:25	LEO	
9 Nov 1999	02:18	LIB		22 Aug 2003	11:35	VIR	
5 Dec 1999	22:41	SCO		15 Sep 2003	15:57	LIB	
31 Dec 1999	04:53	SAG		9 Oct 2003	18:56	SCO	
24 Jan 2000	19:52	CAP		2 Nov 2003	21:42	SAG	
18 Feb 2000	04:43	AQU		27 Nov 2003	01:07	CAP	
13 Mar 2000	11:36	PIS		21 Dec 2003	06:32	AQU	
6 Apr 2000	18:37	ARI		14 Jan 2004	17:15	PIS	
1 May 2000	02:48	TAU		8 Feb 2004	16:20	ARI	

DATE	TIME	SIGN	MOTION	DATE	TIME	SIGN	MOTION
5 Mar 2004	18:12	TAU		8 Oct 2007	06:52	VIR	
3 Apr 2004	14:56	GEM		8 Nov 2007	21:05	LIB	
17 May 2004	22:28	GEM	R	5 Dec 2007	13:28	SCO	
29 Jun 2004	23:15	GEM	D	30 Dec 2007	18:01	SAG	
7 Aug 2004	11:02	CAN		24 Jan 2008	08:05	CAP	
6 Sep 2004	22:15	LEO		17 Feb 2008	16:22	AQU	
3 Oct 2004	17:20	VIR		12 Mar 2008	22:51	PIS	
29 Oct 2004	00:39	LIB		6 Apr 2008	05:35	ARI	
22 Nov 2004	13:31	SCO		30 Apr 2008	13:34	TAU	
16 Dec 2004	17:09	SAG		24 May 2008	22:51	GEM	
9 Jan 2005	16:55	CAP		18 Jun 2008	08:48	CAN	
2 Feb 2005	15:42	AQU		12 Jul 2008	18:38	LEO	
26 Feb 2005	15:07	PIS		6 Aug 2008	04:19	VIR	
22 Mar 2005	16:24	ARI		30 Aug 2008	14:41	LIB	
15 Apr 2005	20:36	TAU		24 Sep 2008	02:59	SCO	
10 May 2005	04:14	GEM		18 Oct 2008	18:30	SAG	
3 Jun 2005	15:17	CAN		12 Nov 2008	15:24	CAP	
28 Jun 2005	05:53	LEO		7 Dec 2008	23:36	AQU	
23 Jul 2005	01:01	VIR		3 Jan 2009	12:35	PIS	
17 Aug 2005	03:04	LIB		3 Feb 2009	03:40	ARI	
11 Sep 2005	16:14	SCO		6 Mar 2009	17:17	ARI	R
8 Oct 2005	01:00	SAG		11 Apr 2009	12:46	PIS	R
5 Nov 2005	08:10	CAP		17 Apr 2009	19:24	PIS	D
15 Dec 2005	15:57	AQU		24 Apr 2009	07:18	ARI	
24 Dec 2005	09:36	AQU	R	6 Jun 2009	09:06	TAU	
1 Jan 2006	20:18	CAP	R	5 Jul 2009	08:22	GEM	
3 Feb 2006	09:19	CAP	D	1 Aug 2009	01:27	CAN	
5 Mar 2006	08:38	AQU		26 Aug 2009	16:11	LEO	
6 Apr 2006	01:20	PIS		20 Sep 2009	13:32	VIR	
3 May 2006	10:24	ARI		14 Oct 2009	22:46	LIB	
29 May 2006	12:41	TAU		8 Nov 2009	00:23	SCO	
24 Jun 2006	00:31	GEM		1 Dec 2009	22:03	SAG	
19 Jul 2006	02:41	CAN		25 Dec 2009	18:17	CAP	
12 Aug 2006	20:20	LEO		18 Jan 2010	14:34	AQU	
6 Sep 2006	06:14	VIR		11 Feb 2010	12:09	PIS	
30 Sep 2006	10:01	LIB		7 Mar 2010	12:33	ARI	
24 Oct 2006	09:57	SCO		31 Mar 2010	17:34	TAU	
17 Nov 2006	08:02	SAG		25 Apr 2010	05:05	GEM	
11 Dec 2006	05:33	CAP		20 May 2010	01:04	CAN	
4 Jan 2007	03:31	AQU		14 Jun 2010	08:49	LEO	
28 Jan 2007	03:32	PIS		10 Jul 2010	11:31	VIR	
21 Feb 2007	08:21	ARI		7 Aug 2010	03:47	LIB	
17 Mar 2007	22:00	TAU		8 Sep 2010	15:44	SCO	
12 Apr 2007	02:14	GEM		8 Oct 2010	07:05	SCO	R
8 May 2007	07:28	CAN		8 Nov 2010	03:05	LIB	R
5 Jun 2007	17:59	LEO		18 Nov 2010	21:18	LIB	D
14 Jul 2007	18:23	VIR		30 Nov 2010	00:33	SCO	
27 Jul 2007	17:28	VIR	R	7 Jan 2011	12:30	SAG	
9 Aug 2007	01:10	LEO	R	4 Feb 2011	05:58	CAP	
8 Sep 2007	16:14	LEO	D	2 Mar 2011	02:38	AQU	

DATE	TIME	SIGN	MOTION	DATE	TIME	SIGN	MOTION
27 Mar 2011	06:52	PIS		10 Dec 2014	16:41	CAP	
21 Apr 2011	04:06	ARI		3 Jan 2015	14:48	AQU	
15 May 2011	22:12	TAU		27 Jan 2015	14:59	PIS	
9 Jun 2011	14:23	GEM		20 Feb 2015	20:05	ARI	
4 Jul 2011	04:16	CAN		17 Mar 2015	10:14	TAU	
28 Jul 2011	14:58	LEO		11 Apr 2015	15:28	GEM	
21 Aug 2011	22:10	VIR		7 May 2015	22:51	CAN	
15 Sep 2011	02:39	LIB		5 Jun 2015	15:32	LEO	
9 Oct 2011	05:49	SCO		18 Jul 2015	22:38	VIR	
2 Nov 2011	08:51	SAG		25 Jul 2015	09:29	VIR	R
26 Nov 2011	12:36	CAP		31 Jul 2015	15:27	LEO	R
20 Dec 2011	18:26	AQU		6 Sep 2015	08:29	LEO	D
14 Jan 2012	05:47	PIS		8 Oct 2015	17:29	VIR	
8 Feb 2012	06:00	ARI		8 Nov 2015	15:30	LIB	
5 Mar 2012	10:24	TAU		5 Dec 2015	04:15	SCO	
3 Apr 2012	15:17	GEM		30 Dec 2015	07:16	SAG	
15 May 2012	14:33	GEM	R	23 Jan 2016	20:31	CAP	
27 Jun 2012	15:07	GEM	D	17 Feb 2016	04:16	AQU	
7 Aug 2012	13:42	CAN		12 Mar 2016	10:23	PIS	
6 Sep 2012	14:47	LEO		5 Apr 2016	16:50	ARI	
3 Oct 2012	06:58	VIR		30 Apr 2016	00:35	TAU	
28 Oct 2012	13:03	LIB		24 May 2016	09:44	GEM	
22 Nov 2012	01:19	SCO		17 Jun 2016	19:38	CAN	
16 Dec 2012	04:38	SAG		12 Jul 2016	05:34	LEO	
9 Jan 2013	04:10	CAP		5 Aug 2016	15:26	VIR	
2 Feb 2013	02:46	AQU		30 Aug 2016	02:06	LIB	
26 Feb 2013	02:02	PIS		23 Sep 2016	14:50	SCO	
22 Mar 2013	03:15	ARI		18 Oct 2016	07:00	SAG	
15 Apr 2013	07:24	TAU		12 Nov 2016	04:54	CAP	
9 May 2013	15:03	GEM		7 Dec 2016	14:51	AQU	
3 Jun 2013	02:12	CAN		3 Jan 2017	07:46	PIS	
27 Jun 2013	17:03	LEO		3 Feb 2017	15:51	ARI	
22 Jul 2013	12:40	VIR		4 Mar 2017	09:09	ARI	R
16 Aug 2013	15:36	LIB		3 Apr 2017	00:25	PIS	R
11 Sep 2013	06:15	SCO		15 Apr 2017	10:18	PIS	D
7 Oct 2013	17:53	SAG		28 Apr 2017	13:13	ARI	
5 Nov 2013	08:42	CAP		6 Jun 2017	07:26	TAU	
21 Dec 2013	21:53	CAP	R	5 Jul 2017	00:11	GEM	
31 Jan 2014	20:49	CAP	D	31 Jul 2017	14:53	CAN	
5 Mar 2014	21:03	AQU		26 Aug 2017	04:29	LEO	
5 Apr 2014	20:30	PIS		20 Sep 2017	01:15	VIR	
3 May 2014	01:21	ARI		14 Oct 2017	10:11	LIB	
29 May 2014	01:45	TAU		7 Nov 2017	11:38	SCO	
23 Jun 2014	12:33	GEM		1 Dec 2017	09:14	SAG	
18 Jul 2014	14:06	CAN		25 Dec 2017	05:25	CAP	
12 Aug 2014	07:23	LEO		18 Jan 2018	01:43	AQU	
5 Sep 2014	17:06	VIR		10 Feb 2018	23:19	PIS	
29 Sep 2014	20:52	LIB		6 Mar 2018	23:45	ARI	
23 Oct 2014	20:52	SCO		31 Mar 2018	04:53	TAU	
16 Nov 2014	19:03	SAG		24 Apr 2018	16:39	GEM	

DATE	TIME	SIGN	MOTION	DATE	TIME	SIGN	MOTION
19 May 2018	13:10	CAN		29 Jan 2022	08:46	CAP	D
13 Jun 2018	21:54	LEO		6 Mar 2022	06:29	AQU	
10 Jul 2018	02:31	VIR		5 Apr 2022	15:17	PIS	
6 Aug 2018	23:27	LIB		2 May 2022	16:10	ARI	
9 Sep 2018	09:25	SCO		28 May 2022	14:45	TAU	
5 Oct 2018	19:04	SCO	R	23 Jun 2022	00:34	GEM	
31 Oct 2018	19:41	LIB	R	18 Jul 2022	01:32	CAN	
16 Nov 2018	10:51	LIB	D	11 Aug 2022	18:29	LEO	
2 Dec 2018	17:01	SCO		5 Sep 2022	04:04	VIR	
7 Jan 2019	11:17	SAG		29 Sep 2022	07:49	LIB	
3 Feb 2019	22:29	CAP		23 Oct 2022	07:51	SCO	
1 Mar 2019	16:45	AQU		16 Nov 2022	06:08	SAG	
26 Mar 2019	19:43	PIS		10 Dec 2022	03:54	CAP	
20 Apr 2019	16:10	ARI		3 Jan 2023	02:09	AQU	
15 May 2019	09:45	TAU		27 Jan 2023	02:32	PIS	
9 Jun 2019	01:36	GEM		20 Feb 2023	07:55	ARI	
3 Jul 2019	15:18	CAN		16 Mar 2023	22:34	TAU	
28 Jul 2019	01:53	LEO		11 Apr 2023	04:47	GEM	
21 Aug 2019	09:06	VIR		7 May 2023	14:24	CAN	
14 Sep 2019	13:43	LIB		5 Jun 2023	13:46	LEO	
8 Oct 2019	17:05	SCO		23 Jul 2023	01:33	LEO	R
1 Nov 2019	20:24	SAG		4 Sep 2023	01:20	LEO	D
26 Nov 2019	00:28	CAP		9 Oct 2023	01:10	VIR	
20 Dec 2019	06:41	AQU		8 Nov 2023	09:30	LIB	
13 Jan 2020	18:38	PIS		4 Dec 2023	18:50	SCO	
7 Feb 2020	20:02	ARI		29 Dec 2023	20:23	SAG	
5 Mar 2020	03:07	TAU		23 Jan 2024	08:50	CAP	
3 Apr 2020	17:10	GEM		16 Feb 2024	16:05	AQU	
13 May 2020	06:45	GEM	R	11 Mar 2024	21:50	PIS	
25 Jun 2020	06:48	GEM	D	5 Apr 2024	03:59	ARI	
7 Aug 2020	15:21	CAN		29 Apr 2024	11:31	TAU	
6 Sep 2020	07:21	LEO		23 May 2024	20:30	GEM	
2 Oct 2020	20:47	VIR		17 Jun 2024	06:20	CAN	
28 Oct 2020	01:41	LIB		11 Jul 2024	16:18	LEO	
21 Nov 2020	13:21	SCO		5 Aug 2024	02:22	VIR	
15 Dec 2020	16:21	SAG		29 Aug 2024	13:22	LIB	
8 Jan 2021	15:40	CAP		23 Sep 2024	02:35	SCO	
1 Feb 2021	14:05	AQU		17 Oct 2024	19:28	SAG	
25 Feb 2021	13:11	PIS		11 Nov 2024	18:25	CAP	
21 Mar 2021	14:16	ARI		7 Dec 2024	06:13	AQU	
14 Apr 2021	18:21	TAU		3 Jan 2025	03:23	PIS	
9 May 2021	02:01	GEM		4 Feb 2025	07:56	ARI	
2 Jun 2021	13:18	CAN		2 Mar 2025	00:36	ARI	R
27 Jun 2021	04:26	LEO		27 Mar 2025	08:40	PIS	R
22 Jul 2021	00:36	VIR		13 Apr 2025	01:02	PIS	D
16 Aug 2021	04:26	LIB		30 Apr 2025	17:15	ARI	
10 Sep 2021	20:38	SCO		6 Jun 2025	04:42	TAU	
7 Oct 2021	11:20	SAG		4 Jul 2025	15:30	GEM	
5 Nov 2021	10:43	CAP		31 Jul 2025	03:56	CAN	
19 Dec 2021	10:36	CAP	R	25 Aug 2025	16:26	LEO	

Venus Tables

DATE	TIME	SIGN	MOTION	DATE	TIME	SIGN	MOTION
19 Sep 2025	12:38	VIR		14 Apr 2029	05:06	TAU	
13 Oct 2025	21:18	LIB		8 May 2029	12:45	GEM	
6 Nov 2025	22:39	SCO		2 Jun 2029	00:10	CAN	
30 Nov 2025	20:13	SAG		26 Jun 2029	15:37	LEO	
24 Dec 2025	16:25	CAP		21 Jul 2029	12:20	VIR	
17 Jan 2026	12:43	AQU		15 Aug 2029	17:06	LIB	
10 Feb 2026	10:18	PIS		10 Sep 2029	10:54	SCO	
6 Mar 2026	10:45	ARI		7 Oct 2029	04:47	SAG	
30 Mar 2026	16:00	TAU		5 Nov 2029	13:38	CAP	
24 Apr 2026	04:03	GEM		16 Dec 2029	23:47	CAP	R
19 May 2026	01:05	CAN		26 Jan 2030	21:33	CAP	D
13 Jun 2026	10:46	LEO		6 Mar 2030	12:50	AQU	
9 Jul 2026	17:21	VIR		5 Apr 2030	09:18	PIS	
6 Aug 2026	19:12	LIB		2 May 2030	06:37	ARI	
10 Sep 2026	08:06	SCO		28 May 2030	03:32	TAU	
3 Oct 2026	07:16	SCO	R	22 Jun 2030	12:23	GEM	
25 Oct 2026	09:09	LIB	R	17 Jul 2030	12:45	CAN	
14 Nov 2026	00:27	LIB	D	11 Aug 2030	05:23	LEO	
4 Dec 2026	08:12	SCO		4 Sep 2030	14:50	VIR	
7 Jan 2027	08:53	SAG		28 Sep 2030	18:33	LIB	
3 Feb 2027	14:30	CAP		22 Oct 2030	18:39	SCO	
1 Mar 2027	06:32	AQU		15 Nov 2030	17:00	SAG	
26 Mar 2027	08:16	PIS		9 Dec 2030	14:51	CAP	
20 Apr 2027	03:56	ARI					
14 May 2027	21:01	TAU					
8 Jun 2027	12:32	GEM					
3 Jul 2027	02:01	CAN					
27 Jul 2027	12:30	LEO					
20 Aug 2027	19:42	VIR					
14 Sep 2027	00:24	LIB					
8 Oct 2027	03:58	SCO					
1 Nov 2027	07:34	SAG					
25 Nov 2027	11:59	CAP					
19 Dec 2027	18:39	AQU					
13 Jan 2028	07:19	PIS					
7 Feb 2028	10:00	ARI					
4 Mar 2028	20:00	TAU					
3 Apr 2028	20:27	GEM					
10 May 2028	23:02	GEM	R				
22 Jun 2028	22:12	GEM	D				
7 Aug 2028	15:25	CAN					
5 Sep 2028	23:17	LEO					
2 Oct 2028	10:07	VIR					
27 Oct 2028	13:51	LIB					
21 Nov 2028	00:57	SCO					
15 Dec 2028	03:38	SAG					
8 Jan 2029	02:46	CAP					
1 Feb 2029	01:02	AQU					
25 Feb 2029	00:03	PIS					
21 Mar 2029	01:03	ARI					

Mars tables

Look up the year you were born and then zero in to find your Mars sign. Full instructions on how to do this are given on pages 30–32.

DATE	TIME	SIGN	MOTION	DATE	TIME	SIGN	MOTION
15 Jan 1955	04:33	ARI		20 Jun 1960	09:04	TAU	
26 Feb 1955	10:22	TAU		2 Aug 1960	04:31	GEM	
10 Apr 1955	23:08	GEM		21 Sep 1960	04:06	CAN	
26 May 1955	00:49	CAN		20 Nov 1960	17:04	CAN	R
11 Jul 1955	09:22	LEO		5 Feb 1961	00:25	GEM	R
27 Aug 1955	10:13	VIR		6 Feb 1961	02:51	GEM	D
13 Oct 1955	11:19	LIB		7 Feb 1961	05:23	CAN	
29 Nov 1955	01:33	SCO		6 May 1961	01:12	LEO	
14 Jan 1956	02:27	SAG		28 Jun 1961	23:47	VIR	
28 Feb 1956	20:04	CAP		17 Aug 1961	00:41	LIB	
14 Apr 1956	23:39	AQU		1 Oct 1961	20:02	SCO	
3 Jun 1956	07:51	PIS		13 Nov 1961	21:50	SAG	
10 Aug 1956	16:18	PIS	R	24 Dec 1961	17:49	CAP	
10 Oct 1956	10:06	PIS	D	1 Feb 1962	23:06	AQU	
6 Dec 1956	11:23	ARI		12 Mar 1962	07:58	PIS	
28 Jan 1957	14:18	TAU		19 Apr 1962	16:58	ARI	
17 Mar 1957	21:33	GEM		28 May 1962	23:47	TAU	
4 May 1957	15:21	CAN		9 Jul 1962	03:49	GEM	
21 Jun 1957	12:17	LEO		22 Aug 1962	11:37	CAN	
8 Aug 1957	05:26	VIR		11 Oct 1962	23:54	LEO	
24 Sep 1957	04:31	LIB		26 Dec 1962	06:11	LEO	R
8 Nov 1957	21:03	SCO		16 Mar 1963	17:21	LEO	D
23 Dec 1957	01:29	SAG		3 Jun 1963	06:29	VIR	
3 Feb 1958	18:56	CAP		27 Jul 1963	04:14	LIB	
17 Mar 1958	07:10	AQU		12 Sep 1963	09:11	SCO	
27 Apr 1958	02:30	PIS		25 Oct 1963	17:31	SAG	
7 Jun 1958	06:20	ARI		5 Dec 1963	09:03	CAP	
21 Jul 1958	07:03	TAU		13 Jan 1964	06:13	AQU	
21 Sep 1958	05:25	GEM		20 Feb 1964	07:32	PIS	
10 Oct 1958	09:46	GEM	R	29 Mar 1964	11:24	ARI	
29 Oct 1958	00:00	TAU	R	7 May 1964	14:40	TAU	
20 Dec 1958	06:46	TAU	D	17 Jun 1964	11:42	GEM	
10 Feb 1959	13:57	GEM		30 Jul 1964	18:22	CAN	
10 Apr 1959	09:46	CAN		15 Sep 1964	05:22	LEO	
1 Jun 1959	02:25	LEO		6 Nov 1964	03:19	VIR	
20 Jul 1959	11:03	VIR		28 Jan 1965	22:38	VIR	R
5 Sep 1959	22:46	LIB		19 Apr 1965	21:56	VIR	D
21 Oct 1959	09:40	SCO		29 Jun 1965	01:11	LIB	
3 Dec 1959	18:08	SAG		20 Aug 1965	12:16	SCO	
14 Jan 1960	04:59	CAP		4 Oct 1965	06:45	SAG	
23 Feb 1960	04:11	AQU		14 Nov 1965	07:18	CAP	
2 Apr 1960	06:24	PIS		23 Dec 1965	05:36	AQU	
11 May 1960	07:18	ARI		30 Jan 1966	07:01	PIS	

DATE	TIME	SIGN	MOTION	DATE	TIME	SIGN	MOTION
9 Mar 1966	12:55	ARI		30 Sep 1972	23:22	LIB	
17 Apr 1966	20:34	TAU		15 Nov 1972	22:16	SCO	
28 May 1966	22:07	GEM		30 Dec 1972	16:12	SAG	
11 Jul 1966	03:14	CAN		12 Feb 1973	05:50	CAP	
25 Aug 1966	15:51	LEO		26 Mar 1973	20:58	AQU	
12 Oct 1966	18:36	VIR		8 May 1973	04:08	PIS	
4 Dec 1966	00:54	LIB		20 Jun 1973	20:53	ARI	
12 Feb 1967	12:19	SCO		12 Aug 1973	14:56	TAU	
8 Mar 1967	17:44	SCO	R	19 Sep 1973	23:19	TAU	R
31 Mar 1967	06:09	LIB	R	29 Oct 1973	22:55	ARI	R
26 May 1967	09:29	LIB	D	26 Nov 1973	00:06	ARI	D
19 Jul 1967	22:55	SCO		24 Dec 1973	08:08	TAU	
10 Sep 1967	01:44	SAG		27 Feb 1974	10:10	GEM	
23 Oct 1967	02:14	CAP		20 Apr 1974	08:18	CAN	
1 Dec 1967	20:11	AQU		9 Jun 1974	00:53	LEO	
9 Jan 1968	09:49	PIS		27 Jul 1974	14:04	VIR	
17 Feb 1968	03:17	ARI		12 Sep 1974	19:08	LIB	
27 Mar 1968	23:43	TAU		28 Oct 1974	07:04	SCO	
8 May 1968	14:14	GEM		10 Dec 1974	22:05	SAG	
21 Jun 1968	05:03	CAN		21 Jan 1975	18:49	CAP	
5 Aug 1968	17:06	LEO		3 Mar 1975	05:31	AQU	
21 Sep 1968	18:38	VIR		11 Apr 1975	19:15	PIS	
9 Nov 1968	06:09	LIB		21 May 1975	08:13	ARI	
29 Dec 1968	22:07	SCO		1 Jul 1975	03:52	TAU	
25 Feb 1969	06:20	SAG		14 Aug 1975	20:46	GEM	
27 Apr 1969	11:24	SAG	R	17 Oct 1975	08:43	CAN	
8 Jul 1969	06:07	SAG	D	6 Nov 1975	12:01	CAN	R
21 Sep 1969	06:35	CAP		25 Nov 1975	18:30	GEM	R
4 Nov 1969	18:50	AQU		20 Jan 1976	21:27	GEM	D
15 Dec 1969	14:22	PIS		18 Mar 1976	13:14	CAN	
24 Jan 1970	21:29	ARI		16 May 1976	11:10	LEO	
7 Mar 1970	01:28	TAU		6 Jul 1976	23:26	VIR	
18 Apr 1970	18:58	GEM		24 Aug 1976	05:54	LIB	
2 Jun 1970	06:50	CAN		8 Oct 1976	20:23	SCO	
18 Jul 1970	06:42	LEO		20 Nov 1976	23:53	SAG	
3 Sep 1970	04:57	VIR		1 Jan 1977	00:41	CAP	
20 Oct 1970	10:56	LIB		9 Feb 1977	11:56	AQU	
6 Dec 1970	16:34	SCO		20 Mar 1977	02:19	PIS	
23 Jan 1971	01:33	SAG		27 Apr 1977	15:45	ARI	
12 Mar 1971	10:11	CAP		6 Jun 1977	02:59	TAU	
3 May 1971	20:57	AQU		17 Jul 1977	15:12	GEM	
11 Jul 1971	06:30	AQU	R	1 Sep 1977	00:19	CAN	
9 Sep 1971	13:51	AQU	D	26 Oct 1977	18:55	LEO	
6 Nov 1971	12:31	PIS		12 Dec 1977	19:12	LEO	R
26 Dec 1971	18:04	ARI		26 Jan 1978	01:59	CAN	R
10 Feb 1972	14:03	TAU		2 Mar 1978	09:56	CAN	D
27 Mar 1972	04:29	GEM		10 Apr 1978	18:49	LEO	
12 May 1972	13:14	CAN		14 Jun 1978	02:37	VIR	
28 Jun 1972	16:08	LEO		4 Aug 1978	09:06	LIB	
15 Aug 1972	00:58	VIR		19 Sep 1978	20:56	SCO	

DATE	TIME	SIGN	MOTION	DATE	TIME	SIGN	MOTION
2 Nov 1978	01:20	SAG		26 Apr 1985	09:12	GEM	
12 Dec 1978	17:38	CAP		9 Jun 1985	10:40	CAN	
20 Jan 1979	17:07	AQU		25 Jul 1985	04:03	LEO	
27 Feb 1979	20:24	PIS		10 Sep 1985	01:31	VIR	
7 Apr 1979	01:08	ARI		27 Oct 1985	15:15	LIB	
16 May 1979	04:25	TAU		14 Dec 1985	18:59	SCO	
26 Jun 1979	01:54	GEM		2 Feb 1986	06:26	SAG	
8 Aug 1979	13:28	CAN		28 Mar 1986	03:46	CAP	
24 Sep 1979	21:20	LEO		8 Jun 1986	23:25	CAP	R
19 Nov 1979	21:35	VIR		12 Aug 1986	07:46	CAP	D
16 Jan 1980	06:18	VIR	R	9 Oct 1986	01:01	AQU	
11 Mar 1980	20:46	LEO	R	26 Nov 1986	02:35	PIS	
6 Apr 1980	08:27	LEO	D	8 Jan 1987	12:20	ARI	
4 May 1980	02:26	VIR		20 Feb 1987	14:43	TAU	
10 Jul 1980	17:58	LIB		5 Apr 1987	16:37	GEM	
29 Aug 1980	05:49	SCO		21 May 1987	03:01	CAN	
12 Oct 1980	06:26	SAG		6 Jul 1987	16:46	LEO	
22 Nov 1980	01:42	CAP		22 Aug 1987	19:51	VIR	
30 Dec 1980	22:30	AQU		8 Oct 1987	19:27	LIB	
6 Feb 1981	22:48	PIS		24 Nov 1987	03:19	SCO	
17 Mar 1981	02:39	ARI		8 Jan 1988	15:24	SAG	
25 Apr 1981	07:16	TAU		22 Feb 1988	10:14	CAP	
5 Jun 1981	05:26	GEM		6 Apr 1988	21:44	AQU	
18 Jul 1981	08:54	CAN		22 May 1988	07:41	PIS	
2 Sep 1981	01:51	LEO		13 Jul 1988	19:59	ARI	
21 Oct 1981	01:56	VIR		26 Aug 1988	14:40	ARI	R
16 Dec 1981	00:14	LIB		23 Oct 1988	22:01	PIS	R
20 Feb 1982	19:13	LIB	R	28 Oct 1988	05:07	PIS	D
11 May 1982	18:35	LIB	D	1 Nov 1988	12:57	ARI	
3 Aug 1982	11:45	SCO		19 Jan 1989	08:11	TAU	
20 Sep 1982	01:20	SAG		11 Mar 1989	08:51	GEM	
31 Oct 1982	23:04	CAP		29 Apr 1989	04:37	CAN	
10 Dec 1982	06:16	AQU		16 Jun 1989	14:10	LEO	
17 Jan 1983	13:10	PIS		3 Aug 1989	13:35	VIR	
25 Feb 1983	00:19	ARI		19 Sep 1989	14:37	LIB	
5 Apr 1983	14:03	TAU		4 Nov 1989	05:29	SCO	
16 May 1983	21:43	GEM		18 Dec 1989	04:56	SAG	
29 Jun 1983	06:53	CAN		29 Jan 1990	14:10	CAP	
13 Aug 1983	16:54	LEO		11 Mar 1990	15:53	AQU	
30 Sep 1983	00:11	VIR		20 Apr 1990	22:08	PIS	
18 Nov 1983	10:25	LIB		31 May 1990	07:10	ARI	
11 Jan 1984	03:19	SCO		12 Jul 1990	14:43	TAU	
5 Apr 1984	12:22	SCO	R	31 Aug 1990	11:39	GEM	
19 Jun 1984	18:17	SCO	D	20 Oct 1990	19:30	GEM	R
17 Aug 1984	19:50	SAG		14 Dec 1990	07:45	TAU	R
5 Oct 1984	06:02	CAP		1 Jan 1991	12:49	TAU	D
15 Nov 1984	18:08	AQU		21 Jan 1991	01:15	GEM	
25 Dec 1984	06:37	PIS		3 Apr 1991	00:48	CAN	
2 Feb 1985	17:19	ARI		26 May 1991	12:19	LEO	
15 Mar 1985	05:06	TAU		15 Jul 1991	12:36	VIR	

Mars Tables

DATE	TIME	SIGN	MOTION	DATE	TIME	SIGN	MOTION
1 Sep 1991	06:38	LIB		18 Dec 1997	06:36	AQU	
16 Oct 1991	19:04	SCO		25 Jan 1998	09:26	PIS	
29 Nov 1991	02:18	SAG		4 Mar 1998	16:17	ARI	
9 Jan 1992	09:46	CAP		13 Apr 1998	01:04	TAU	
18 Feb 1992	04:37	AQU		24 May 1998	03:42	GEM	
28 Mar 1992	02:04	PIS		6 Jul 1998	08:59	CAN	
5 May 1992	21:35	ARI		20 Aug 1998	19:15	LEO	
14 Jun 1992	15:55	TAU		7 Oct 1998	12:28	VIR	
26 Jul 1992	18:58	GEM		27 Nov 1998	10:10	LIB	
12 Sep 1992	06:05	CAN		26 Jan 1999	11:59	SCO	
28 Nov 1992	23:31	CAN	R	18 Mar 1999	13:41	SCO	R
15 Feb 1993	07:43	CAN	D	5 May 1999	21:32	LIB	R
27 Apr 1993	23:40	LEO		4 Jun 1999	06:11	LIB	D
23 Jun 1993	07:42	VIR		5 Jul 1999	03:59	SCO	
12 Aug 1993	01:10	LIB		2 Sep 1999	19:29	SAG	
27 Sep 1993	02:15	SCO		17 Oct 1999	01:35	CAP	
9 Nov 1993	05:29	SAG		26 Nov 1999	06:56	AQU	
20 Dec 1993	00:33	CAP		4 Jan 2000	03:00	PIS	
28 Jan 1994	04:05	AQU		12 Feb 2000	01:04	ARI	
7 Mar 1994	11:01	PIS		23 Mar 2000	01:25	TAU	
14 Apr 1994	18:01	ARI		3 May 2000	19:18	GEM	
23 May 1994	22:36	TAU		16 Jun 2000	12:29	CAN	
3 Jul 1994	22:30	GEM		1 Aug 2000	01:20	LEO	
16 Aug 1994	19:14	CAN		17 Sep 2000	00:19	VIR	
4 Oct 1994	15:48	LEO		4 Nov 2000	02:00	LIB	
12 Dec 1994	11:31	VIR		23 Dec 2000	14:37	SCO	
2 Jan 1995	21:27	VIR	R	14 Feb 2001	20:05	SAG	
22 Jan 1995	23:48	LEO	R	11 May 2001	16:08	SAG	R
24 Mar 1995	17:18	LEO	D	19 Jul 2001	22:45	SAG	D
25 May 1995	16:09	VIR		8 Sep 2001	17:50	CAP	
21 Jul 1995	09:20	LIB		27 Oct 2001	17:19	AQU	
7 Sep 1995	06:59	SCO		8 Dec 2001	21:52	PIS	
20 Oct 1995	21:02	SAG		18 Jan 2002	22:53	ARI	
30 Nov 1995	13:57	CAP		1 Mar 2002	15:04	TAU	
8 Jan 1996	11:01	AQU		13 Apr 2002	17:35	GEM	
15 Feb 1996	11:49	PIS		28 May 2002	11:42	CAN	
24 Mar 1996	15:12	ARI		13 Jul 2002	15:23	LEO	
2 May 1996	18:16	TAU		29 Aug 2002	14:37	VIR	
12 Jun 1996	14:42	GEM		15 Oct 2002	17:57	LIB	
25 Jul 1996	18:31	CAN		1 Dec 2002	14:26	SCO	
9 Sep 1996	20:01	LEO		17 Jan 2003	04:23	SAG	
30 Oct 1996	07:12	VIR		4 Mar 2003	21:16	CAP	
3 Jan 1997	08:10	LIB		21 Apr 2003	23:48	AQU	
6 Feb 1997	00:37	LIB	R	17 Jun 2003	02:25	PIS	
8 Mar 1997	19:49	VIR	R	29 Jul 2003	07:37	PIS	R
27 Apr 1997	19:09	VIR	D	27 Sep 2003	07:52	PIS	D
19 Jun 1997	08:29	LIB		16 Dec 2003	13:23	ARI	
14 Aug 1997	08:42	SCO		3 Feb 2004	10:04	TAU	
28 Sep 1997	22:22	SAG		21 Mar 2004	07:39	GEM	
9 Nov 1997	05:32	CAP		7 May 2004	08:45	CAN	

DATE	TIME	SIGN	MOTION	DATE	TIME	SIGN	MOTION
23 Jun 2004	20:50	LEO		15 Jan 2011	22:41	AQU	
10 Aug 2004	10:14	VIR		23 Feb 2011	01:05	PIS	
26 Sep 2004	09:15	LIB		2 Apr 2011	04:51	ARI	
11 Nov 2004	05:10	SCO		11 May 2011	07:03	TAU	
25 Dec 2004	16:03	SAG		21 Jun 2011	02:49	GEM	
6 Feb 2005	18:31	CAP		3 Aug 2011	09:21	CAN	
20 Mar 2005	18:01	AQU		19 Sep 2011	01:50	LEO	
1 May 2005	02:57	PIS		11 Nov 2011	04:15	VIR	
12 Jun 2005	02:29	ARI		24 Jan 2012	00:54	VIR	R
28 Jul 2005	05:12	TAU		14 Apr 2012	03:53	VIR	D
1 Oct 2005	22:04	TAU	R	3 Jul 2012	12:31	LIB	
10 Dec 2005	04:03	TAU	D	23 Aug 2012	15:24	SCO	
17 Feb 2006	22:43	GEM		7 Oct 2012	03:20	SAG	
14 Apr 2006	00:59	CAN		17 Nov 2012	02:36	CAP	
3 Jun 2006	18:43	LEO		26 Dec 2012	00:48	AQU	
22 Jul 2006	18:52	VIR		2 Feb 2013	01:53	PIS	
8 Sep 2006	04:18	LIB		12 Mar 2013	06:25	ARI	
23 Oct 2006	16:37	SCO		20 Apr 2013	11:48	TAU	
6 Dec 2006	04:58	SAG		31 May 2013	10:58	GEM	
16 Jan 2007	20:54	CAP		13 Jul 2013	13:22	CAN	
26 Feb 2007	01:32	AQU		28 Aug 2013	02:05	LEO	
6 Apr 2007	08:49	PIS		15 Oct 2013	11:04	VIR	
15 May 2007	14:06	ARI		7 Dec 2013	20:41	LIB	
24 Jun 2007	21:26	TAU		1 Mar 2014	16:23	LIB	R
7 Aug 2007	06:01	GEM		20 May 2014	01:31	LIB	D
28 Sep 2007	23:54	CAN		26 Jul 2014	02:24	SCO	
15 Nov 2007	08:25	CAN	R	13 Sep 2014	21:56	SAG	
31 Dec 2007	16:00	GEM	R	26 Oct 2014	10:42	CAP	
30 Jan 2008	22:33	GEM	D	4 Dec 2014	23:56	AQU	
4 Mar 2008	10:01	CAN		12 Jan 2015	10:20	PIS	
9 May 2008	20:19	LEO		20 Feb 2015	00:11	ARI	
1 Jul 2008	16:21	VIR		31 Mar 2015	16:26	TAU	
19 Aug 2008	10:03	LIB		12 May 2015	02:40	GEM	
4 Oct 2008	04:33	SCO		24 Jun 2015	13:32	CAN	
16 Nov 2008	08:26	SAG		8 Aug 2015	23:32	LEO	
27 Dec 2008	07:30	CAP		25 Sep 2015	02:17	VIR	
4 Feb 2009	15:55	AQU		12 Nov 2015	21:40	LIB	
15 Mar 2009	03:19	PIS		3 Jan 2016	14:32	SCO	
22 Apr 2009	13:44	ARI		6 Mar 2016	02:28	SAG	
31 May 2009	21:18	TAU		17 Apr 2016	12:14	SAG	R
12 Jul 2009	02:55	GEM		27 May 2016	13:51	SCO	R
25 Aug 2009	17:15	CAN		29 Jun 2016	23:38	SCO	D
16 Oct 2009	15:32	LEO		2 Aug 2016	17:49	SAG	
20 Dec 2009	13:26	LEO	R	27 Sep 2016	08:06	CAP	
10 Mar 2010	17:09	LEO	D	9 Nov 2016	05:51	AQU	
7 Jun 2010	06:11	VIR		19 Dec 2016	09:22	PIS	
29 Jul 2010	23:46	LIB		28 Jan 2017	05:38	ARI	
14 Sep 2010	22:37	SCO		10 Mar 2017	00:33	TAU	
28 Oct 2010	06:47	SAG		21 Apr 2017	10:31	GEM	
7 Dec 2010	23:48	CAP		4 Jun 2017	16:15	CAN	

DATE	TIME	SIGN	MOTION	DATE	TIME	SIGN	MOTION
20 Jul 2017	12:19	LEO		13 Feb 2024	06:04	AQU	
5 Sep 2017	09:34	VIR		22 Mar 2024	23:47	PIS	
22 Oct 2017	18:28	LIB		30 Apr 2024	15:32	ARI	
9 Dec 2017	08:59	SCO		9 Jun 2024	04:34	TAU	
26 Jan 2018	12:56	SAG		20 Jul 2024	20:42	GEM	
17 Mar 2018	16:40	CAP		4 Sep 2024	19:46	CAN	
16 May 2018	04:55	AQU		4 Nov 2024	04:09	LEO	
26 Jun 2018	21:04	AQU	R	6 Dec 2024	23:33	LEO	R
13 Aug 2018	02:13	CAP	R	6 Jan 2025	10:43	CAN	R
27 Aug 2018	14:05	CAP	D	24 Feb 2025	02:00	CAN	D
11 Sep 2018	00:55	AQU		18 Apr 2025	04:20	LEO	
15 Nov 2018	22:20	PIS		17 Jun 2025	08:35	VIR	
1 Jan 2019	02:19	ARI		6 Aug 2025	23:23	LIB	
14 Feb 2019	10:51	TAU		22 Sep 2025	07:54	SCO	
31 Mar 2019	06:12	GEM		4 Nov 2025	13:01	SAG	
16 May 2019	03:09	CAN		15 Dec 2025	07:33	CAP	
1 Jul 2019	23:19	LEO		23 Jan 2026	09:16	AQU	
18 Aug 2019	05:18	VIR		2 Mar 2026	14:15	PIS	
4 Oct 2019	04:21	LIB		9 Apr 2026	19:35	ARI	
19 Nov 2019	07:40	SCO		18 May 2026	22:25	TAU	
3 Jan 2020	09:37	SAG		28 Jun 2026	19:28	GEM	
16 Feb 2020	11:32	CAP		11 Aug 2026	08:30	CAN	
30 Mar 2020	19:43	AQU		28 Sep 2026	02:48	LEO	
13 May 2020	04:17	PIS		25 Nov 2026	23:36	VIR	
28 Jun 2020	01:45	ARI		10 Jan 2027	12:59	VIR	R
9 Sep 2020	22:22	ARI	R	21 Feb 2027	14:13	LEO	R
14 Nov 2020	00:36	ARI	D	1 Apr 2027	14:08	LEO	D
6 Jan 2021	22:26	TAU		14 May 2027	14:47	VIR	
4 Mar 2021	03:29	GEM		15 Jul 2027	05:40	LIB	
23 Apr 2021	11:48	CAN		2 Sep 2027	01:51	SCO	
11 Jun 2021	13:33	LEO		15 Oct 2027	23:13	SAG	
29 Jul 2021	20:32	VIR		25 Nov 2027	18:37	CAP	
15 Sep 2021	00:13	LIB		3 Jan 2028	16:01	AQU	
30 Oct 2021	14:20	SCO		10 Feb 2028	16:31	PIS	
13 Dec 2021	09:52	SAG		19 Mar 2028	19:35	ARI	
24 Jan 2022	12:52	CAP		27 Apr 2028	22:21	TAU	
6 Mar 2022	06:22	AQU		7 Jun 2028	18:20	GEM	
15 Apr 2022	03:05	PIS		20 Jul 2028	20:09	CAN	
24 May 2022	23:17	ARI		4 Sep 2028	14:35	LEO	
5 Jul 2022	06:03	TAU		24 Oct 2028	01:10	VIR	
20 Aug 2022	07:56	GEM		21 Dec 2028	08:46	LIB	
30 Oct 2022	13:26	GEM	R	14 Feb 2029	08:16	LIB	R
12 Jan 2023	20:56	GEM	D	7 Apr 2029	13:09	VIR	R
25 Mar 2023	11:45	CAN		5 May 2029	19:00	VIR	D
20 May 2023	15:31	LEO		5 Jun 2029	04:48	LIB	
10 Jul 2023	11:40	VIR		7 Aug 2029	16:02	SCO	
27 Aug 2023	13:19	LIB		23 Sep 2029	08:13	SAG	
12 Oct 2023	04:03	SCO		4 Nov 2029	00:31	CAP	
24 Nov 2023	10:14	SAG		13 Dec 2029	05:24	AQU	
4 Jan 2024	14:57	CAP		20 Jan 2030	10:27	PIS	

DATE	TIME	SIGN	MOTION
27 Feb 2030	19:06	ARI	
8 Apr 2030	05:26	TAU	
19 May 2030	09:28	GEM	
1 Jul 2030	15:19	CAN	
15 Aug 2030	23:55	LEO	
2 Oct 2030	09:41	VIR	
21 Nov 2030	07:54	LIB	

Resources

Part one

The astronomy of Venus and Mars

Online

Many websites tell you what's in the sky above your head at your location, so you'll know when Venus and Mars are visible. Here are a few to get you started:

HEAVENS ABOVE: https://www.heavens-above.com/main.aspx

HM NAUTICAL ALMANAC OFFICE: http://astro.ukho.gov.uk/nao/sky_general.html

IN THE SKY: https://in-the-sky.org/location.php

SKY AND TELESCOPE: https://skyandtelescope.org/observing/interactive-sky-chart/

SKYVIEW CAFÉ: https://skyviewcafe.com/#/

If you want to know about the astronomy of Venus and Mars, the NASA website is invaluable:

VENUS: https://nssdc.gsfc.nasa.gov/planetary/planets/venuspage.html

MARS: https://nssdc.gsfc.nasa.gov/planetary/planets/marspage.html

Books

If you don't know your way around the constellations in the night sky and can't tell Bootes from the Big Dipper, these books will help:

Heifetz, Milton D. and Tirion, Wil. *A Walk through the Heavens*. 4th edition. Cambridge University Press, 2017

Dunlop, Storm and Tirion, Wil. *Guide to the Night Sky*. Collins. This book is published annually, giving a month-by-month guide to the night sky in the coming year, but make sure you buy the correct one for your country.

Part two

Your astrological toolkit

Online

Several websites will calculate your birth chart free of charge but they won't interpret it for you unless you pay.

ASTRODIENST: https://www.astro.com/horoscope

ASTROLOGY.COM: https://www.astrology.com.tr

ASTROSEEK: https://horoscopes.astro-seek.com/birth-chart-horoscope-online

The above birth chart calculators will convert a time to UT/GMT but this site will do it, too.

GREENWICH MEANTIME: https://greenwichmeantime.com

Astrology software

If you want to take astrology to the next level, there will inevitably come a time when you need to invest in an astrology program, whether it's for your computer or your phone, so you can calculate charts in an instant. There are plenty to choose from but it's best to start with something simple and easy to use. Your choice may be determined by whether you use Windows or macOS. Many astrology programs will give you brief interpretations of the charts you've calculated. Here are two of the best.

ASTROGOLD: https://www.astrogold.io

TIMEPASSAGES: https://www.astrograph.com/astrology-software/

Books

Clifford, Frank C. and Graham, Fiona. *The Astrology of Love, Sex and Attraction,* Flare Publications and The London School of Astrology, 2005

Kirby, Babs and Stubbs, Janey. *Love & Sexuality: An Exploration of Venus and Mars,* Element, 1992

Struthers, Jane. *Moonpower,* Eddison Books, 2019

Struthers, Jane. *Write Your Own Horoscope,* White Lion Publishing, 2021

Tompkins, Sue. *The Contemporary Astrologer's Handbook,* Flare Publications and The London School of Astrology, 2006

Index

A

B

C

D

E

F

G

H

I

J

L

M

R

S

T

U

V

W

Z

About the author

Jane Struthers is a professional astrologer, tarot reader, palmist and homeopath. She has written more then 30 non-fiction books on a wide variety of topics that include astrology, tarot, and her bestselling *Red Sky at Night*, on the British countryside. She is the weekly astrologer for *Bella* magazine, and regularly lectures on astrology and the tarot. Find her at www.janestruthers.com

Acknowledgements

This book first came to life on 30 August 2019. When I looked later, I realized that the astrology was perfect, as Venus and Mars were sitting either side of the new Virgo Moon (see page 7 for the chart). Many thanks to Lisa Dyer, who originally gave the thumbs-up to *Your Love Stars* and set it on the initial steps of its path to publication; to Kate Pollard who became its later guide; and to Wendy Hobson for her eagle-eyed editing skills. Thanks also to everyone else at Welbeck who worked on this book. I must also thank Chelsey Fox, my fabulous agent, and Bill Martin, my wonderful husband, for their behind-the-scenes help and support. Final mentions go to Sophie, who gave me daily feline encouragement by alternately sitting on my lap and walking across my keyboard to do some spontaneous editing, and her brother Hector who preferred to snooze on the carpet by my feet.